TREE TALK AND TALES

TREE TALK AND TALES

Daniel H. Henning, Ph.D.

ISBN: 1-4033-7003-6 (electronic)
ISBN: 1-4033-7004-4 (softcover)

Library of Congress Control Number: 2002095150

This book is printed on acid free paper.

Printed in the United States of America
Bloomington, IN

1stBooks – rev. 10/28/02

CONTENTS

PART TWO

TREE TALES

WILDERNESS SPRUCE

Dedication

This book is dedicated to the trees and forests of the world and to their efforts in spiritual awareness to educate human beings, including myself, so that present and future generations of all living beings will have their intangible and tangible blessings.

It would be impossible to acknowledge the countless individuals worldwide who have helped and influenced me in my efforts to get closer to trees and forests and to their protection. I also dedicate this book to these individuals and to those like them who love the trees and forests as the living, spiritual beings that they are.

INTRODUCTION

Part One of this volume consists of messages "spoken" to me by trees and forests in Thailand, Australia, Montana, Norway, and Canada during my journeys over the past 12 years. Part Two involves tree tales and legends from Buddha and Asian countries, Nepal, Celtic countries, and Finland which I found during these same journeys. Part Three, "Wilderness Spruce," is a tree novella (for the young and older) that I wrote in Montana.

I believe that there is an aura of mystery and spirituality about trees (and other living beings for that matter) which we do not understand and simply must accept. There is an old story of two Buddhist monks who meditated under a tree in Tibet for several hours. Finally, one monk turned to the other and said, "And they call that a tree."

Trees are living bridges which connect Mother Earth and Father Sky in living processes and sacredness. They are vulnerable, silent, and noble with "eyes" that can see that which we cannot. I believe that they have a consciousness and intelligence that goes beyond our understanding as they commune with the earth and the cosmos in their Oneness and diversity. It is this sacred perception that enables them to see so deeply into life, including the inner life of human beings. They are in a perpetual state of meditation and awareness through their living tissues above (trunk, branches, and leaves or needles) and below (root systems) the earth.

Although trees are individuals and vary in their receptivity and responsiveness to "talking," I believe that they are basically concerned with the survival and quality of all life, including human beings. They also realize, I believe, that they need human beings who are wise, clear, and dedicated to their earth home. In this sense, trees have a wisdom, spirituality, and desire to help and to educate human beings along Deep Ecology lines.

Deep Ecology can be considered to include the spiritual dimensions of the environmental movement. It asks deeper and more personal questions that get at the real causes (such as ignorance and greed) behind issues as well as the "place," values, ecological limits, etc. Deep Ecology recognizes Homo sapiens as a single species in the integrity of the ecosystem or universe, along with other numerous species of plants and animals, and their interaction.

This Deep Ecological awareness is basically spiritual in nature. It recognizes that other forms of life on earth (and hence their well being) have intrinsic value and inherent worth, regardless of their "usefulness" to people. It further recognizes that human beings are only one particular strand in the web of life and calls for a paradigm shift from anthropocentric to ecocentric. Deep Ecology calls for change in values and spiritual perspectives.

The following public statement is "The Deep Ecology Platform" by Arne Naess and George Sessions, two eco-philosophers:

> 1. The well-being and flourishing of human and nonhuman life on Earth have value in themselves (synonyms: inherent worth, intrinsic value). These values are independent of the usefulness of the nonhuman world for human purposes.
> 2. Richness and diversity of life forms contribute to the realization of these values and are values in themselves.

3. Humans have no right to reduce this richness and diversity except to satisfy vital needs.

4. Present human interference with the nonhuman world is excessive, and the situation is rapidly worsening.

5. The flourishing of human life and cultures is compatible with a substantial decrease of the human population. The flourishing of nonhuman life requires such a decrease.

6. Policies must therefore be changed. The changes in policies affect basic economic, technological structures. The resulting state of affairs will be deeply different from the present.

7. The ideological change is mainly that of appreciating the life quality (dwelling in situations of inherent worth) rather than adhering to an increasing higher standard of living. There will be a profound awareness of the difference between big and great.

8. Those who prescribe to the foregoing points have an obligation directly or indirectly to participate in the attempt to implement the necessary changes.

The ecocentric approach of Deep Ecology, with its call for responsible self and society correction, correlates directly with the basic ideals of Buddhism. Ignorance and greed, problems that cause anthropocentrism, are transformed by a new movement in values and perspectives. The result is a paradigm shift that find equal value and reverence for all life forms, including trees. Protecting biodiversity becomes a way of life, not a conflict.

Deep Ecology calls for deep changes in the way we relate to the environment and its living beings, including trees, ourselves, and our institutions. Current efforts through domestic and foreign funding, government programs, legislation, NGOs (non-governmental environmental organizations), science and technology are not working to protect the trees and forests, let alone the environment, at home or abroad.

This is particularly true of tropical forests which are rapidly being destroyed and degraded. Tropical forests are the richest and most diverse expression of life that has evolved on earth. Irreversibly, tropical forests are literally disappearing within our lifetimes. Most tropical forests are too complex and their species too diverse to regenerate themselves. So their destruction can be considered permanent and irreversible.

At the same time, old growth trees in northern forests may require centuries to "come back" to their original size and complexity after being "harvested," i.e., logged. So these forests and their vulnerable ecology can also be considered ruined after logging for all practical purposes. Harvesting timber, sustainable yield, and reforestation are simply public relations myths and platitudes generated by the lumber industries and government agencies to make the logging business more acceptable.

Obviously, something much different is needed to stop these destructive patterns along with "new" ways of relating to trees and forests. More people are now looking at the potential of spiritually-based solutions which might address the underlying values and causes of environmental imbalance.

These spiritual solutions offer us guidance along previously chartered paths that will help us accomplish the shifts in self-centered and anthropocentric world views that we have been stuck in for the millennia. We need to re-educate ourselves along ecocentric lines to the intrinsic worth of all life, including trees, for its own sake instead of its worth to us as humans.

Buddhism is one of these spiritual paths that has been practicing the values and tenets of Deep Ecology for over 2,500 years. In Part One, some of the Asian trees that spoke to me exemplified this spiritual connection between Buddhism and Deep Ecology as did the Asian tree tales in Part Two. Buddha was born, meditated, enlightened, taught, and died under trees and in forests where he spent most of his life. Could the Buddha nature be based on enlightenment through the tree nature? Besides Buddha's teachings of loving kindness and compassion for all beings, one of first rules was to forbid monks from cutting living trees.

In a personal conversation, Shaman Malidoma Patrice Some, Ph.D. recently told me that his African tribe, the Dagara, consider trees to be the highest and most intelligent forms of life because of their abilities to communicate meanings without words on the highest, clearest, and most spiritual level, i.e., through silence. Next would come animals which make sounds and noises that have some meanings for interpretation. Last of all would come human beings who use words and languages that fail to communicate clearly the meanings, understandings, and spiritual essences to others. Consequently, human beings would be relegated to the lowest level with animals next and finally trees at the highest level of life and nature. Perhaps we have much to learn from trees, particularly as we observe the meanings of the world around us.

BACKGROUND

Beyond this background section, Part One consists only of what trees have "said" to me in several countries over the past 12 years.

It goes without saying that one needs to get the ego and its projections and illusions out of the way when listening to what individual trees or groups of trees in a forest try to communicate. I had noticed over the years that I sometimes thought I "heard" trees. This "heard" interaction, however, was not audible like a human voice. It was more of a sense of having "heard" a message, talk, or a poem in my heart, body, and lastly, mind.

It would appear a bit arrogant and anthropocentric to believe that trees would talk in the English of human beings. I believe they have their own language(s) and hence adapted their communication so I could "hear" their voiceless voices in English. Maybe if I were German, they would have spoken to me in German.

Although trees are individuals and vary in their receptivity and responsiveness to "talking," I believe that they are basically concerned with the survival and quality of all life, including human beings, besides their own lives. They also realize that they need human beings who are wise, clear, and dedicated to their earth home and its life. In this sense, trees have a wisdom, spirituality, and desire to help and educate human beings about nature and the world, that is very similar to the teachings of Deep Ecology.

For that reason, I thought it would be a good idea to write down their messages and teachings for Deep Ecology. I have written down only what the trees actually indicated to me in the most honest and exact form possible or as the Buddhists say, "as it is." As a professional environmental activist, I did have the intention of bringing out some Deep Ecology messages and teachings by trees for the benefit of their protection.

I have always loved trees and wanted to protect them as long as I can remember. In fact, I can still remember myself as a twelve year old boy crying and yelling as I unsuccessfully tried to stop a bulldozer from destroying a beautiful small forest in our Garfield Height suburb in Ohio. The bulldozer operator yelled back something about a housing development and progress as he continued to knock down the trees. But I still wanted that beautiful forest and its trees to be the way they had been. At that early age, I resolved to do something about protecting trees and nature.

So I became a conservationist, then an environmentalist, and finally, a Deep Ecologist to that end. With this dedication of protecting trees and wilderness, I studied biology, ecology, forestry, and conservation of natural resources besides social sciences as an undergraduate and graduate student at three universities. During summers, I worked as a park ranger naturalist in national parks or as a wilderness ranger in national forests.

After receiving a Ph.D. in political science and forestry from Syracuse University, I started my teaching career at Montana State University, Billings, while trying to be a wilderness advocate and environmental scholar (to the annoyance of many conservative faculty and administrators). I married, had two great kids (Tundra and Forest), got divorced after a 20 year marriage, and took early retirement to do something for tropical forest protection in Asia.

For the past twelve years, I served as a Senior Fulbright Research Scholar (one year) and as a United Nations Environmental Consultant and Trainer in South East Asia with a focus on tropical forests, protected areas, biodiversity, and Deep Ecology. I also did volunteer work in these areas, including for the National Park Divisions of Thailand and Queensland, Australia and for the Division of Nature and Wildlife Conservation, Forest Department, Myanmar (Burma). I took up Buddhism while in Thailand and often lived in Buddhist forest monasteries. I continue to work with protecting trees and wilderness areas worldwide as a consultant, trainer, and volunteer. These activities include my offering a workshop on, "Buddhism and Deep Ecology," relative to forest protection.

Yet, in all the above activities, I knew that I had to personally change just as much as those who exploit, destroy, and degrade the trees and forests. Clearly, the need in my life has been deep change, just as Deep Ecology calls for deep changes in the way we relate to nature and other living beings. I do my best to work twelve step programs and have had countless hours of psychotherapy and New Age/holistic health workshops and programs in efforts to find some peace in my life. The saving grace has been my spiritual path with God, friends, Buddhism, and, quite frankly, trees.

Before deep changes of this nature (both personal and Deep Ecology) can occur, it is necessary to deal with the personal aspects, projections, and illusions of the individual. The individual psyche or soul needs to heal so that the way is clear for healing the relationships between the human being and other living beings, including trees and forests. This healing includes getting the ego with its fears, illusions, and projections out of the way, i.e., letting go.

Thus one's Buddha Nature, Christ Spirit, Higher Power, or whatever one chooses to call one's spiritual life, can come through in acceptance, love, and compassion for one's self and for life.

It also means letting go of the mind and getting into the heart.

This is particularly difficult for an academic like myself who has mostly lived in the mind due to fear over the years.

It means listening with the heart and body and, then, the mind.

This listening goes well beyond the negative and judgmental thoughts of self and others. The clear and uncluttered mind perceived through the heart and body provides the consciousness that is so badly needed for personal and Deep Ecology changes. Much of this consciousness can only come through awareness of our thoughts, emotions, and actions so we can have this clarity of our spiritual nature. More often than not, we need to understand and clear our personal illusions and hangups (or defilements as the Buddhists would say) before we can really understand the full meaning of Deep Ecology messages. Meditation helps a lot in this process as well as listening to nature.

Thus an ego-free consciousness must first be developed through awareness practices before messages from a tree or the collective voice of a forest can be heard, and their meanings correctly intuited. As the old adage goes: "Heal Thyself," before healing or understanding others. This healing, in turn, requires the helping hands of spirituality and wisdom to become the heart of love and compassion through awareness and mindfulness.

Consciousness becomes the link, the bridge, the breakthrough between trees and forests and the sea of emotions and mind of our human nature. It becomes the escape and release from the entrapment of separateness and fragmentation. It becomes the path for uniting with the ecological flow of life beyond the apparent illness and fragmentation of the ego with its illusion and projection. This tree healing moves one into a flowing biodiversity with all aspects of Oneness, Deep Ecology, wisdom, and love, and the immediacy of the here and now.

Consequently, much of my tree talks for change centers on issues personal to me, but that directly and indirectly relate to Deep Ecology and to all living beings, including collective humanity. Deep Ecology messages are also, directly and indirectly, intertwined throughout the tree talks.

There is a great deal of mysterious wisdom and spirituality about nature, particularly trees, which may be speaking for the collective voice of Gaia (the earth as a living and intelligent organism), the cosmos, or the divine. This spirituality can be defined in terms of relationships with ourselves, with other living beings, with the earth, with the cosmos, and with our Higher Power. With their silence and stillness, trees can speak personal and Deep Ecology messages which reach our inner core, our true nature, our Buddha, Christ, divine nature or whatever we choose to call it in terms of these relationships.

This "speaking" is basically a sacred process which transforms and changes our finite, imprisoned consciousness to one more associated with the infinite, the metaphysical, and the multidimensional. It does require the letting go of past and future concerns and being in the here and now where the living trees and forests are trying to reach us.

It is in this opening up to the present or "nowness" with awareness that enables one to really connect with one's own spiritual nature and with that of the tree or forest. This means releasing our illusions and projections as well as accepting the mystery involved without trying to understand or analyze it. It is a sacred interaction that reaches our deeper and infinite nature as well as brings in the diversity, wisdom, and creativity of trees and forests.

While doing some of the field work for this book in Australia, I first met with Michael Roads, the author of TALKING WITH NATURE and JOURNEY INTO NATURE. I asked him for any advice that he might wish to give me on my efforts to talk with trees. His points were: (1) meditate on the tree(s), (2) have a responsibility for the experience and truth of what the tree said, (3) watch dialogue in that it is easy and subtle to convey where you are with a dialogue in your mind (I have basically avoided dialogue), (4) watch ego. You can come too much from intellect–need to bring in the heart not the mind, (5) need not interpret or identify species of trees (mind concern), and, (6) do not mix up ego with messages from the tree.

In other meetings and workshops with Michael, I have had some excellent teachings and experiences on expanding my consciousness to gain a sense of Oneness and to look within for the real source and sense of self on a multidimensional and metaphysical basis.

In an old letter of 12/12/90, Michael wrote, "My relationship with Nature is rather metaphysical–beyond the physical–and beyond a physical nature there is a vast and powerful movement in consciousness. The paradox is–what is happening in Nature and our environment is perfect; equally, people like you who attempt to address the environmental problems, add to that perfection. It is a matter of intent. Intent is of immense power, it precipitates action. If the basis of action is fear, then nothing, I repeat nothing happens in the consciousness of Nature, other than sowing the seeds of more fear. If, however, the intent is based on love–then the connection with all life is breathtaking."

When I asked about naming the trees by species, Michael advised that this was not important, but that the message from the tree(s) was important. I did breathe a sigh of relief because of my lack of knowledge of Australian and Thai tree species. Consequently, I have decided to simply assign appropriate names or areas to trees and forests relative to their messages and talks.

Agreeing with Michael's point on tree species, Fr. John Kirsh, a spiritual naturalist who loves Yellowstone National Park and who seeks the divine in nature, says, "My failure in retreats is when I use my rational mind to attempt to know the unknowable. Species are more real when we simply experience them without trying to label or define them. Therefore, don't spend too much time identifying plants and animals and rocks by name. Too much occupation with remembering the past and thinking about the future kills the mystic within us. Forget the idea of naming everything you see and some day for a brief moment you will experience divinity."

Much of my past work in the environmental field, quite frankly, has centered on fear and ego- fear of myself, fear of forests being destroyed, fear that I could not do anything to stop this destruction. And, finally, using my fear to alert and enrage the public and environmental groups into action as well as threatening and exposing the "enemy" bureaucrats, politicians, and private company executives with anything that they might fear or have revealed.

My ego came into the picture by trying to get self-approval and to blame through activism and scholarly works. After all, it was my noble battle to protect trees, forests, wilderness, and the environment. I would write countless letters to the editors of newspapers, politicians, and bureaucrats, participate in public and protest meetings, confront decision makers, work with environmental organizations, present papers, write articles (even law articles so they would have some teeth), and books, give talks, teach environmental classes and workshops, and anything else that I could dream up.

Like other environmentalists, I did accomplish a lot in efforts to bring out the real issues and to protect and promote nature. Yet, I was into my mind on most of this ego and fear=based work for the environment with intellectual efforts and arguments outside, and emotional pain and fear inside. At the same time, there were and are increasing and unending threats and battles (old and new) for environmental destruction was almost everywhere.

Worldwide, nationally, and locally, government and industry has the money, time, red tape, lawyers, communications, and experts to back up unwise developments and exploitations in economic and environmental controversies. So it was no wonder that most environmentalists and I were angry, depressed, and "burned out" much of the time. It was like trying to shovel sea water against an incoming ocean tide.

I knew I had a lot of ecological and environmental truth on my side as did other activists. But it made little difference in my makeup or confidence in an endless and overwhelming battle, particularly for a workaholic like myself. There was a lot of intellect and fear, but not love. My heart was there for the trees, but it was buried somewhere in fear and ego. There was very little of the love or good intent which Michael had indicated. But there was a lot of self=hate and blame.

However, with more focus on Deep Ecology and spirituality, I began to see that things had to change, particularly after a lot of personal crises in my life. I realized that I had to find spiritual answers and approaches. I became more and more aware that the trees were trying to tell me something–if only I would pay more attention to them instead of my personal issues and illusions.

At first, I thought I would be listening mainly for Deep Ecology messages from the trees. But I increasingly found that the majority were of a personal nature. Yet, I felt that much of this "personal nature"could apply to most people. It was important to clarify and release these personal issues before attempting to understand the Deep Ecology messages in a clear and meaningful way.

I started to write down what I felt I had heard in my heart, body, and lastly mind from a given tree or group of trees in a forest. At first, it was just some notes for my own personal edification. But, later, as the messages developed, I thought I should share the tree talk or messages in the form of a book.

The fact that the "voiceless voices" of the trees and forests in this book had to use words in English to communicate with this human being would certainly point toward limitations with the complexities and individual interpretations of these words and the true meanings that the silent trees and forests were trying to convey. As noted, I have done my best to record only what the trees and forests have indicated to me without additions, projections, or interpretations.

Much of this tree talk experience in the field and later writing has been very important for change in my life. It has helped me to grow in awareness, consciousness, spirituality and to bring more sensitivity and perspective into my personal life and into my Deep Ecology work in trying to protect trees which I feel is my mission in this life. And, most important, it has brought me closer to the trees and forests that I love as well as to myself. So I can now see and feel them more as the living, spiritual, sentient beings that they are–wise, wonderful, and full of life, love, wisdom, and compassion.

At this point, I will present the tree talk as it was presented to me by the trees and forests in several countries without interpretations or "trying to make it sound better." The tree talk chapters will simply be categorized by country and/or chronologically. It is my hope that this tree talk will be of value in your own personal and Deep Ecology life as it was and is in mine.

CHAPTER ONE

THAILAND AND AUSTRALIA

WAT DHAMMAKALA PANA TREE BY POND

(1) How dare you try to define, dictate, or manipulate relationships with other people. They are uncontrollable and unpredictable by you and your influences–and even beyond God's pushing His/Her will on people. In similar fashion, other people cannot influence, manipulate, or control you unless you let them. Put these things in God's hands and grace. Let God's will grant us peace on earth.

(2) Stop being so silly–let your light shine through. Behave appropriately and recognize that all suffer. God wants you to be happy and so do you.

(3) Let go of your grievances. Recognize that you are one with your karma and others have their karma–as well as blessings.

(4) Sit up straight. Be a friend to yourself. Who knows your situation better and what is good for you than you? God and you understand and love you as a friend–be yourself.

(5) I am the Holy Tree Spirit–you must command your soul to give up its grievances, its grief–to let the light flow through you inside and outside as you release your grief–bitterness–so you can really be yourself. You must command it and it will respond to God's will which will clear your will. You have a choice to command your soul and spirit and to stop being silly and spending your life on grieving and blaming, manipulation, and anger. Be yourself for God's sake. His will is your will.

(6)
Trees of God
Trees of Life
Be with me
For I am dedicated to thee
throughout the rife
and everything nice in life
I do reflect trees are perfect
Be here now
In my life
I love you trees
We are trees
Trees are we
And Oneness with thee
It is great to be a tree

(7) You must live for us–stay alive. Notice how your perceptions and consciousness change. Notice how we stay all bent with the breeze and wind as you must. Be flexible, be wholeness, be good (God). You have a job. Stay in life, pursue it, do it. Drop the bullshit.

(8) Give love and forgiveness without attachments, not manipulating, without trying to please to gain self approval–just like the breeze. Give what you really are for giving's sake.

(9) Life is joy. Be happy. Lovable when you smile–smile for God and us trees. And tell God light and love.

(10) I can't tell you anything. I am merely a channel for God and His/Her Holy Spirit. Take my gifts of observing, calmness, and poise for your work. I am the perfect tree for you–scraggly branches and leaf clumps of different shades of green–and compare with the lush green neighbor tree. I am like you–different, divine, diverse. Do not judge but enjoy the variety, the difference, the uniqueness. Enjoy your uniqueness and awareness and Oneness, particularly in relationship to yourself and life.

(11) Breathing in and breathing out with carbon dioxide for me and oxygen for you we actually and symbolically complete our Oneness with air and spirit. By the way, I am a female tree. All my intentions are in this flow. Be aware for you are alive and, at times, don't know it. Have a response and intentions to the ecology of life as it flows with you. Be there–not somewhere else–for this is the only ecological moment there is, and you need to be aware of it fully, or it floats by like ships in the night. This means giving up attachments and all thoughts that keep you from fully being here. Be here with me a tree so you can get love from us and protect us as we help you to grow and to do your protection of light and love for God's sake and God's glory.

(12) You take things too personally. When you get personally hurt, you must remember that you usually get what you asked for–with your mind committee based on your accumulated karma and conditioning to another's mind committee. You mix your deep ecology into all this mind stuff. Then add the economic and political forces which have no moral or ethics. So your ego with its

blame, compulsions, need for approval, and other emotional stuff naturally comes out as you try to influence people, places, and things that are pretty much out of control. So you end up feeling hurt and powerless.

My advice is: let the Holy Spirit guide you and let go. Forgive what they have done to you on an ego basis. Look at some of my branches and leaves which have been physically hurt. Everyone hurts in some form as individuals. Put your consciousness and focus on the Oneness–the big picture with forests being destroyed and devastated. You can do something about this hurt to forests in new ways to protect them. So let go of all your petty hurts. They are not personal and simply come from conditioning of yourself and others. Don't be so intense–trying to so hard constantly. Just relax–let flow. Be yourself and listen to your spirit.

(13) What about me a tree–just equal–not your inferior–not your superior–just your fellow living being in the total scheme of things. I give you my natural and spiritual blessings and you give me your goodness and yourself in nature. I am a tree being and you are a human being. But together we are intertwined in many physical, emotional, and spiritual ways to marvel at our ecology and to blend in the whole. We are just living beings who live and love. We are just what we are, nothing more and nothing less. May God be blessed for we are so. We are brothers and sisters–you and me, the tree.

In the ecosystem, earth, cosmos, spiritually we are energy connected to life with vibrations. We are impermanent, rising, existing, and falling away. You are me, a tree, and I am you, a human. In many ways, we really are the same. So why do you humans destroy us to meet your *wants*, not needs, and to satisfy your endless craving. You need us. We do not need you. Yet we are the same as you–living beings who just want to live and be happy. Vulnerable we are. Divine we are just like you. So protect us for trees we are.

(14). Be ecocentric and observe, not egocentric. Be aware and patient with peace and wisdom. Be effortless, effecting your actions with perspective and love and compassion. Oneness comes with the removal of your ego-self.

(15) By trying to control your interactions and relationships with others and a sick ecosystem, you are living in a world of fear, illusions, anger, and depression. Thus the ego blocks itself and unhappily cuts itself off from the reality of life which is and wants to be wild and free. So let loose your controls and manipulations of the outside and just be yourself inside. Go with the flow. Be flexible and bend with the wind like my branches and leaves do.

(16) Listen to the Holy Spirit. Let the Holy Spirit guide you. Stop trying to do too much too quick. Do what you can in a time flow in harmony and recognize the impermanence of everything and your priorities will change. Do not create endless clutter and sankara of bad experiences which drain your energy and peace. Enjoy life–release. Things will get done as they are supposed to. Keep it simple and trust God.

(17) No ego, no self, no I, no me, no mine. This is the way we trees are. We are aware. This is what you really want–to be ecocentric, not egocentric as you usually are. To be fully alive, free, in life and ecology instead of imprisoned by your ego. How can you really interact with all life this way? How can you love and respect other human beings when your thoughts, words, and actions are centered on your ego with its human centered wants and demands, let alone needs. How can you recognize the spiritual, intangibles, mysteries, wonders of life. What you see, hear, smell, feel, and touch all relate to your ego and illusions–so it is not really real to begin with.

Look at me. I am a collective voice and expression of all trees. I am an individual–just like every living being and its individual parts are individuals. Just like my every leaf is individual and unique. Yet I am non-self and see you as you really are: non-self. So let loose of your illusions of having a self. You are merely aggregates in process. So be yourself by recognizing your non-self in Oneness. And, in this recognition, you gain your identity in common with all life and Oneness. You are an integral and unique part of this Oneness just as I am–and in living communication with it.

(18) You tend to humiliate yourself a lot. There is a difference between humiliation and being humble. Humus means soil–of the earth and alive. But when you humiliate yourself, you place yourself beneath earth life with degradation of being and soul. All of this is simply an illusion by your ego that accumulates to attack yourself. Much of this is due to your failure to recognize life as equanimous and constantly changing.

You are equal to all forms of life, including all humans, by the simple fact that you are alive. You have the dignity and spirituality of all life of the creation. So why do you mourn and grieve that you are not equal or better than other forms of life, particularly other human forms. Why not be like me, a tree, noble–with dignity– with my own intrinsic value while not having to prove myself? When you humiliate yourself, inside or outside, you lose respect and love for yourself as do others.

I venture to say that a lot of tree killers have this self-hatred that goes with humiliation. They want to kill and destroy so they can feel superior to overcome their sense of inferiority and inequity. And what is easier to destroy or degrade than a vulnerable tree that cannot run away? But you attack yourself. So stop this silly game. We trees need you to protect us.

(19) Consider Buddha and trees. He was born under a tree, meditated and lived under trees, enlightened under a tree, taught the Dhamma under trees, and died under a tree. Why were the trees necessary and vital for Buddha and his followers? To be around trees and nature?

Could Buddha have been enlightened through a tree acting as

a channel from the cosmos? Could the all-encompassing Dhamma have passed through trees to provide him with his enlightenment and wisdom while meditating and open from the blocking ego with its illusions, cravings, and aversions—so that he might be closely connected with the cosmic channel through us trees?

RAINFOREST EDGE AT EAGLE HEIGHTS RETREAT CENTER, TAMBORIE MOUNTAINS, QUEENSLAND, AUSTRALIA

(20) We trees can see with eyes that you humans do not have. We can perceive things you simply are incapable of perceiving. This may include invisible forms like fairies, devas, and other things which most human beings cannot pick up. You might be able to sense some these things. We can also hear things that you cannot hear.

With your human projections and languages, you may not always understand what we are trying to communicate to you as well as the reverse. However, keep trying. We trees need to develop as many connections and understandings with you humans as possible—for our own protection as well as for all life on the planet. We need to develop a new interconnected, spiritual consciousness which transcends all of life on a multidimensional and metaphysical basis.

RAINFOREST WALK AT EAGLE HEIGHTS RETREAT CENTER

(21) (Old stump) There is too much stuff in your world. Too much clutter. Too much information. Too much holistic/spiritual stuff. So you become fragmented and desperate under time and place pressure and not really being where you are—the present moment, forgetting all about your purpose in life and what your spiritual journey is.

So here we are in oneness. As an old stump, I reflect on the

shortness of life as well as its oneness. Look at the trees that sur-
round me. Be there in Oneness. Reflect on interrelatedness, the
freshness and space of us in your life. Be with us. Just be like us—
open and responsive to nature. Do not try so hard to do everything–relax–and be yourself. Keep your deep ecology messages
simple, clear, concise. Keep it simple.

(22) Palm trees by a river. In this beauty, this magnificence,
how can you worry about what somebody did to your glasses?
Look at the shadows of green lights on us palms. The glare of the
big trees. The birds singing. See the Oneness. Be alive. Be part of
us. For you are a part of us. You are in us and we are in you. Be
aware. Be alive.

Let the negative thoughts go through you. They are impermanent just like positive thoughts. Keep your mind upon we trees.
Be yourself.

(23) Rainforest on the other side of the river. You can't control
us, so why try? You humans try to manage and manipulate the
forest with everything torn up at the end–just like you try to control everything outside. Let your mind just be. Simply allow, accept, feel, and be, for your life as well as for the forest. We trees are
here to help you, but we must be free–free to be what we are–just
as you are free on your path, regardless of efforts. We are trees–
wild and free and you are yourself. So relax and go with the flow.
Be happy and free and let all life be happy and free.

(24) Eucalyptus on the upper trail. So you don't like us because of our bad reputation in Asia. But do not condemn us. Embrace us for we live. We are here in our native home–ecological and
spiritual. Do not condemn us or yourself or anything for that matter.
Look at our beautiful and tall bodies in forest, our bark like smooth
skin, and green leaves. Accept and enjoy us for we are what we are.
Stop judging us with your mind and open your heart. Just relax

and be yourself. Accept the wholeness of love and nature. The Oneness of all things.

(25) Palm on the upper trail. Be calm–like a palm. Notice my beautiful white flowers which you did not even know were there. Observe and be aware–get your mind off you and your ego stuff. So you can look at all the flowers of life. Rest in the spiritual and talk to the Holy Spirit inside and outside. For you are with us and will always be. So relax and be calm like a palm–and enjoy life as it is by being aware.

(26) Rainforest on the upper trail. We are all incomparable so do not judge or compare yourself or anything with others. Don't compare your images with them and what you apparently see as good or bad or better or worse than yourself for that matter. So you should not compare one tree with another. We are all good as living beings and have a right to our existence–to carry on our struggle for survival just as you do.

SAL TREES IN FOREST AT KLONG NATIONAL PARK, THAILAND

(27) I spread my arm branches to you in openness, love, and peace. Open yourself to the intelligent order on earth of the universe. Let it flow in love and support as you serve to protect we trees.

(28) Look as the wind flows and blows through tree branches and learn. Like a holy, moving spirit–undulating and rising and falling away–like the Buddhist impermanence of change which permeates all of life. See the flow amidst us–note how flexible we are as we sway back and forth with the movements. Do the same with your life–go with the flow as you make the changes–the rising and falling away. When you are too stiff, too influenced, too dogmatic–from your ego and attachments–to the way you want

things to be and to stay that way, you really suffer and make others suffer too.

You cannot control the winds of change so why try? Let nature be nature. Let life be life. Let wind be wind. Let trees be trees. Let people be people. And let yourself be yourself. Do not get angry, sad or whatever with the winds of change. Be glad for the freshness and winds which enliven and bring newness to all life.

(29) It's all love. Do not let your ego or threshold stop you from enjoying life. Be glad that you are a part of sharing life and messages of change. Let your emotions all flow through the mind with compassion and loving-kindness. Have gratitude for our symbiosis and for your part and service in protecting trees. Have gratitude to God that you were chosen for this work.

(30) We were made for you and you were made for us–to love and protect each other. We love you unconditionally and will never abandon you. Feel the our spirit reaching, touching, and connecting with you. Feel our spirit reach into your sense of darkness. Tell it to heal as a powerful Holy Spirit of love and light drives out darkness of negativity, fear, abandonment, and other illusions which separate you from your loving awareness of God–within and without.

(31) Feel this healing spirit. We are together and change will be. We ask that you be in the moment. Release your negative thoughts so you can be open and aware and so we can reach you with our love, compassion, and healing. We are channels between Mother Earth and Father Sky. This is the Holy Spirt for you. Listen to it. Be with it. Be with our unconditional and healing love.

(32) Feminine/masculine, monoecious/dioecious, human/tree. What difference does it make? We are all equals. Living beings. Why dichotomize Oneness?

(33) Why do you come to our trees in this forest place? Why do you feel more spiritual, compassionate, alive, and peaceful here? Why do you love life more here? You are with us and aware of us. Could it be because you really feel connected with what you call nature in us? Could it be because you really feel a part of the community of life–of Oneness–when you are really in the present moment? And can this feeling be transformed spiritually to a caring and protecting of this living community, including the trees which bring you here?

(34) We are a cosmic channel–a spiritual bridge between Father Sky and Mother Earth. Honor trees for we reflect heavenly forms of beauty, utility, and spirituality. Protect us from destruction and degradation for we deserve this dignity as sacred and living life forms on earth.

(35) Be alive. Be aware, be patient, be a tree like me poised and straight to meet fate vulnerable and dignified for life is to be risked and tried; so it is to be a tree

(36) Be in atonement and tone your life. We help you with wisdom as you already know. But apply it to your living.

TREE IN BANGKOK

(37) I am as I am. Just be just as I am. Stop trying to be something you may or may not be. Just as God made you instead of something else for outside acceptance or approval. Be inside and just be you.

(38) Look at my different shades of green in my leaves–as the light and shadows intermingle to bring out my colors, forms, and beauty.

CHAPTER TWO

THAILAND

SAL TREE BY POND AT DHAMMAKALA MONASTERY (Thailand, 1997)

(1) Oneness–you are a part of me–I am a part of you–as we exchange my oxygen for your carbon dioxide. You breathe in my oxygen and breathe out your carbon dioxide. I breathe in your carbon dioxide and breathe out my oxygen. You are not separate or a fragmented self, but an inter connected and essential Oneness with life. Give up self serving and selfishness.

(2) Don't talk so much. Be careful with words and the thoughts behind them. They can have powerful effects on yourself and other living beings.

(3) Don't judge (some leaves are a bit shabby while the next tree has very green leaves) and accept me as you accept yourself.

This is true spiritually–self acceptance and acceptance of others as they are.

(4) Pay attention–not half assed–forget random thoughts–observe–be attentive and focus on life right now.

(5) Be a listening professor–listen to trees.

(6) Be grateful–and full to the moment–to life. Feel the flows/sensations in my tree body and your human body–rising and falling as impermanence dictates–up and down–tree and you.

(7) Be creative in everything. It is your claim to immortality and spirituality.

(8) Unworthiness:

> (a) Which of my leaves is the most unworthy–the most worthy? They are all part of me with their own uniqueness.
>
> (b) Observe my dead, brown leaf falling to the ground with the other dead, brown leaves already on the ground by my trunk. Which is the most worthy and the most unworthy among these dead leaves. They are all dead in whatever previous life form. And the same applies to you and other humans. So live now.
>
> (c) You compare me with surrounding trees–which is the most worthy? Comparison kills. Each has its own unique points, advantages, and disadvantages.
>
> (d) Notice the bees in my branches–like thoughts–impermanent, rising and falling away–like sensations–like our breathing and exchanges of oxygen and carbon dioxide.
>
> (e) Your experiences–which you consider worthy or unworthy–were necessary to get you where you are today.

"Bad" or "Good" but you would not be who and where you are without them.

(f) Your obsessing on unworthiness or grandiosity is a way of egoism and arrogance for insisting on special entitlements, attention, and sympathy, but it ends up in your feeling apart, isolated, and fragmented from wholeness and life.

(g) Just be like me, a tree–and only God can make a tree–and you.

(h) Self-accept and self-love yourself as part of nature. You cannot really love anyone or anything unless you accept and love yourself.

(i) I Am a spirit/deva, so listen and absorb and be–practice. The Holy Spirit speaks through me–listen.

(9) You have a right to be here as I do. And you must be content and believe in life and its various forms to really be alive and survive.

(10) The essence of life, with its vibrations and sensations, is in both of us as in all life. It is a common bonding for connections, communications, and communion in Deep Ecology and spirituality.

(11) You need to meditate by me and other trees to release your defilements, aversions, cravings, and ignorance and to really get at the depth of Deep Ecology, love, and life and what you and others can do to protect life, including trees.

(12) Spirituality is the key. The Holy Spirit for you and his/her many manifestations, particularly trees.

(13) By observing the impermanence of everything rising and falling and by defenselessness with dignity and spirituality, you

will do much good for Deep Ecology protection of us–by getting at the real causes and solutions in a creative and spiritual manner.

(14) Let go of illusions and defilements and stay in the present moment.

(15) We offer each other love, forgiveness, compassion, sympathetic joy–these are the things of real importance and of nurturing life.

(16) You talk with trees through God and the Holy Spirit. What more could you want for a sacred gift?

(17) You cannot stop negative thoughts and feelings from emerging anymore than I can stop a leaf from falling. But like me, let it go; don't cling or attach to them. Just accept them and their impermanence like Yin and Yang or the mosaic of life.

(18) Be grateful for life. Be open to receive just as my branches and leaves are spread to receive the sunlight–open, expectant, and flowing–this is being part of nature and Oneness in life.

(19) Deep Ecology means being deep and spiritual, like my roots sinking deep into Mother Earth.

(20) Have expectancy and patience toward life. Let things unfold. Observe, without expectations, control, forcing.

(2l) I am the Holy Spirit/Tree Spirit for you in this form. Listen and be.

(22) Have patience. Look at how I silently and patiently I am as a tree. Just be–be patient.

(23) Have dignity and intimacy with yourself. It isn't necessary to tell all and everything–which ruins things.

(24) Be ordinary. Be equanimous toward life's rising and falling—a real part of nature with demands or specialness.

(25) You are one of us and one with us. And you had better help us. Protect us.

BANGKOK TREES (Late December, 1997 and early January, 1998)

(26) Ragged tree in street. In the polluted sky, I still turn my branches and leaves upward. Can you see some of my leaves dying? Yet I survive. I have a life and am grateful.

(27) Tree at Pantip Court. Look how I orient myself toward the sun in what you humans call tropism—I am simply responding to nature. Why do you humans often move away from sunlight or the enlightenment in your lives? Could it be because of your illusions and clinging and artificiality which bring you toward darkness and bondage rather than light? Why not be natural and free and respond to nature?

(28) Sal tree in Lupini Park. Be here now—in the present moment or be a half-ass in the past or future fantasies. You cannot connect with nature and life when your mind is somewhere else. Open up and be authentic with me and life by being here now. Not somewhere else.

(29) Large, old tropical tree at American Embassy. Do not thrust yourself upon me like an intruder. Approach me slowly and with dignity and respect for I am an elder. I will be happy to let my love, warmth, and beauty flow upon you. Feel the energy in my large trunk with your hands. It flows of life of the earth and connects us ecologically and spiritually.

CHAPTER THREE

AUSTRALIA

(1) Tree at Meditation Point at Eugella National Park, Queensland, Australia

Do not lose your magnificence–your grandeur and aliveness–your real and natural creatureliness. Love it is; see this in us. See silence in nobility and nobility in silence. See how gripping we are for your heart and soul. We are life and appeal to the inner you–your solid something as a whole. Is your being not a part of things instead of your psychological hangups? You are one of us and we love you. You have this creatureliness about you as a creation of God. You were put here by God as one his creations with us.

(2) We are incomparable. So do not judge/compare yourself or anything with others. Everyone has their skills, ideas, shortcomings. But don't compare your uniqueness, strengths and weaknesses with others. So you should not compare one tree with another or one living being with another. We are all of God and have a right to carry on our struggle for existence each day we are alive

without being judged or compared. We are free, living spirits and incomparable.

(3) Mackay Tulip Oak at Eugella National Park (creation hike).

Stay with us instead of being separate and alone. Feel our vibrations, sensations. Feel our diverse and beautiful shades of green and shimmering of our leaves. We connect you–channel you to the universe of the cosmos. We are here for you and you are here for us. So be upbeat as our leaves and branches blow. We love you and you love us. We ground you and center you in Mother Planet Earth while reaching you tall and straight with leaves above. We are you and you are us- a sacred oneness forever. We reach for you– so open and be as we a tree. Sacred and magnificent soil and soul. We are your loving home everywhere.

(4) To really be yourself, you must be like a tree unbound. Here and now in the moment. Not in illusions of past or future, but right here and now, rooted and grounded, yet connected to all of nature in oneness and awe. Feel these good vibrations and sensations of life that you have found yourself in love with in God's Nature, so that it really can be the *you* that God lives to love and serve. So be a tree like me–no culls–be there.

(5) Die to your illusions and ego. Let your feminine, softer side emerge. Rise into balance between your masculine and feminine. Transform sacredly as you bring this process into wholeness, ecologically, and reflect to the life that is in all nature.

(6) Understory trees–old but small. We lie under the canopy and the mid level trees. Waiting and watching for an opening in the sun. Some of my brothers and sisters may be 30, 40, or many more years, yet very small in height and width but with large leaves to catch the limited sunlight that does get through. Bound up by the big trees, we wait silently and patiently for the opening that may or may not come. When a big tree or its branches fall, it leaves an opening for sunlight as well as for nutrition for us to

shoot up rapidly into the open niche. For nature abhors a vacuum and we have waited long for these opportunities to be what we are supposed to be–big trees. But, alas, only a few of us will get this opportunity. Most of us will spend our lives bound as ground cover, yet very much alive and part of the forest family.

(7) Ode to Tree Stump. In the rainforest, I sit as a stump. A reminder of bygone days when they took many trees of primary growth. I was one of them. I sprouted and grew into a beautiful tree, gorgeous, full, and complete–at home with the forest. Now I am a stump.

(8) (The following are from the rainforest areas in general rather than specific trees) Don't be afraid to admit that you love life and that you need to be more conscious of the creation of all life. Tree forms, water flowing, green branches, powerful.

(9) Creation Creek. When you enter the forest, try not to forget that you are entering a sacred place of trees and spirits. Although you may not see us, you can sense and feel us. We are spirit and we know you. Noble and beauty- our loveliness and depth. We are here and now. Living forms of trees and spirits who have a special affinity for you. The grace in love in spirit and in truth.

(10) Wishing point. Wish to be whole to be in harmony and balance and God in nature to serve. To fill your spiritual faith and to really be the soul that you are—outside as well as inside. To be for God in trees and nature forever.

(11) Creation Creek area..Vibrations and sensations and electric magnetic currents connect you naturally–internally and externally–to the force-field of my tree energy of the forest of ecology of interaction and interdependence as a large part of the Oneness. The flow of Creation Creek calls your internal self-energy. Feel a part of it, be a part of it–a spoke in the web of the tree forest

vibrations and sensations in energy, in deep peace, and in balance. Given illusions of separateness and conflict, relax; let go and live, for you are in the energy flow of life–deep, peaceful, here, now, spiritual, and together. With the sun coming down over the brown river while it flows in the surroundings of a magnificent rainforest–all connected to God–you don't have to get approval and justification or fear anyone. Become who you are–spiritually, mentally, physically, and emotionally as a manifestation of God and trees.

(12) Notice my biodiversity. Notice the variety of my trees and plants. Notice the color, form, shades of my leaves, the sharp and slight contrasts, the mosaic of my spirit forms—visible and invisible, the brown soil, the layer of leaves and how they blend into my forest ecology. You have my permission to be here, do good, serve by recognizing biodiversity in yourself and others.

(13) Disappointments and regrets? You think that you are often frustrated, disappointed, and hurt in your efforts to do something for the rainforests (and yourself as well). Yet consider us. How much we are reduced from the large old growth rainforests of the region by the pioneers (who called us scrub) to small pockets here and there among agriculture, roads, and developments. Think of all the losses of spirits, species, and life forms of trees and rainforests. Feel this hurt, this loss, this pain, this senseless destruction of good, old growth trees as the land is cleared. Feel the vulnerability and losses and hurt and grinding wrath and greed of the pioneer neighbors.

Stop playing God. Stop judging God's time. Look at it through God's eyes and compassion for human folly. God's time and plan—not yours, but do the best you can. Love God, trees—and the rest will follow.

(14) Do you feel sad about the destruction and degradation? What are you going to do now? Pick up on our essence of life forms to be sensitive and caring to those who might be able to help in

our protection. Do not despair over your defeats and the poor decisions by organizations and people when they could have done for us. Or the vast amount of corruption and manipulation rampant in tropical forest governments along with the many so-called experts. It is wasted.

Rather be brave, accept reality, and the wisdom and love to do what you can at the moment in time–for God and forests for trees and all the living forms in nature, including leaves. You do not have to give in to ignorance–which is really ignoring–or to greed and aversion.

(15) What a beautiful, spiritual feeling and energy flow from the forest land and trees–how gripping and moving it is. We displace ego, suffering, and misery with deep-felt joy. Do you understand why it is important to protect us–just like the aborigine–spiritual yet destroyed? Keep using your heart and mind. Stay open to our essence as you connect with us. Do not lose us or the great gift to survive and enjoy the life you love through God with His Grace to the glory of God. God is your protector and our protector.

(16) You constantly want understanding, approval, and acceptance from everyone. Yet we understand you and love you. People do not understand each other. There is the mystery and whole complexity of one's being. There is also the spiritual you. Be yourself as we do. God's loving beings.

(17) You are our protection. You have been given the gift of channeling us. What more do you want. Just be yourself and open your heart and mind and connect with us and your consciousness. You have been chosen to communicate our spiritual messages- to protect the trees and forests of planet earth. This is your service, this is your life. Do not worry about pleasing anyone or gaining their approval. Just do it for God and yourself in love, spirit and

truth for your real essence of life. God bless you. We love you and always will.

(18) Tree covered with strangler fig. Look at me–a tall tree, yet mostly covered with a strangler fig which has vines all over my trunk. The vines first started when a bird let its droppings with fig seeds fall on me. Suddenly they grew and bound my upper trunk and started to strangle me while sending down their own branches. I am like many of you humans–bound and strangled by your conditioning and karma of life. Yet, I am still vibrant and willing and free to follow life as it is.

(19) Tree with large growth at top. Notice the beautiful and majestic platform of staghorn ferns and orchid leaves which make up the lotus-like seat in my top branches. I am sure that even Buddha would gladly meditate in it. In fact, Buddha nature sits in my throne of orchid lilies and is surrounded by a cloudlike mysterious holy vapor. He looks over the green rainforest from my high post and is filled with eternal peace and serenity in the rainforest through deep meditation. Nature is Buddha nature in my tree in Oneness.

(20) General rainforest by Sky View area. Listen- you humans had to think we are apart from you, non-spiritual and worthless in our present form in order to cut us down. The Australian pioneers could not destroy the Aborigines, despite their spiritual, ritualistic, and non-violent nature, unless they took them as non-human objects without individuality. The Aborigines are spiritual beings who relate to plants, animals, and other living things. And they have the right to their struggle for survival as all living things, not to mention the forest spirits, visible and invisible. Need to embrace.

(21) We are not what you think we are and you are not what you think you are—non-self. So do not discount us or delegate us to separateness and infractions. We are the living link to your broth-

ers and sisters in Indians and Aborigines. In a tree and nature we are all equal in dignity–human or non-human in form. Give up your illusions and delusions about us and look at us realistically in nature. You destroy us as well as yourself if not attuned with life and spirituality of all beings.

(22) I am Gunyan, but in birth I am the clouds and moisture as a cloud forest dense. Time and space mean nothing as I go with the earth rising and falling. And equanimous toward all. Feel the sensations and vibrations of the earth in its natural rhythms–that grace, truth, and logic. We reflect it–the universal, divine intelligence and order for the cosmos–life itself. You get in the atonement with the rhythm of life. Why not meditate and release ego so you can really be with us? We love you beyond words, time and space through the mysterious and mystic of our Oneness and spirituality where you are a part and parcel of us. So be conscious of the way–and be–be a tree.

(23) Forest valley by Sky View. Look at healthy forests as natural forests. Look at the sick and degraded forests and what used to be forests, like the cleared land around the sugar cane. Like the human Aids disease, it does not kill but reduces and destroys the immune system to destroy the health and ecology of a person or forest. Destroy and degrade the forests and Aids takes over the rest of the sickening process. Protect us in protected areas; keep us alive and healthy and away from Aids-type invasions of our energy and spirit.

(24) Sky in forest. Look how rainy and dark we are at times–look how spotted with bright sunlight, look how cloudy and windy. But regardless of this water, weather, or other conditions, do try to look deeper into the understanding that, just as each tree is an individual, so can each individual forest have different moods as you do, individually and collectively: sad, happy, angry, and so on. We have our moods just as you do. The thing to keep in mind

is impermanence–rising and falling away. This too will pass away whether good or bad. So be sensitive and compassionate to us and be aware of the larger context. Be with us in accepting and letting go while changing with the forest, and you will flow on. We do a lot for our tree brothers and sisters who live here and who are being redirected.

(25) Palm trees and Tree Ferns. Right here, you are ready as ever. You do not have to look for purposes, for secret wisdom and knowledge. You have the amazing gift of talking with trees and channeling trees and their spiritual messages. You are a unique being and a loving child of God with a service to protect trees and to help and inspire people to understand and love and protect them in the spiritual universe. A Right On fight for the forest and for the trees now–worthy and with spirit. Be ordinary without illusions to really be yourself.

(26) Permean Palm. Cloud forest trail. Always harmonious. Always ask for our tree blessings when in the forest. These are my places and spirituality in the forest. Some trees may be negative for you. Ask my permission/blessings and you will be protected and blessed and opened to the response. It is sacred land that you enter–show it proper reverence for life as you enter. Just as you ask permission to enter other homes, seek my permission. Ask and it is usually given. Be sensitive to the spirits of the forest and your interaction for we are all vulnerable.

(27) Permean Palm. There are spirits in the forest for it is a spiritual place. A place of energy and diversity and different forms– all kinds of spirits, visible and invisible, positive and negative, healthy and unhealthy–so be aware when you enter. Protect your- self and ground yourself with conscious contact with your higher power. Be one with the earth and flow through rather than con- flict and confront. Accept and honor the spirits, trees, and forests. Respect their individuality. Some are open and friendly, some are

neutral, some are inhibited, some want to be alone, some are angry—they are all individuals, different and changing. They may be
angels, devas, fairies, and other spirits of the forest. Since they are
forest spirits, they need the forest to live in. When the forest is
destroyed, they are destroyed.

(28) Small tree in understory. I am just a small tree on the
forest floor. Some of us may be 30 years or more and a quarter of an
inch in width and 3 feet high. We are below the dominant trees
and middle level trees so very little sunlight travels down to us.
Our leaves are unusually large to catch it when it finally reaches
the bottom level of the forest floor. Patiently, we wait for an opening—bright, shiny, and headed for the sky if the opportunity pre-
sents itself when a tree falls. If it does not, we struggle trying to get
as much sunlight as we can by twisting and turning our branches
and leaves toward the sunlight. Regardless, we are ready for the
challenges of life with light and love and to go forth magnificently
and in Oneness.

(29) General rainforest. Ego and tree spirit, we are restoring
you and protecting you from your silliness, from your dumb and
error-prone ego, and we are transforming you in this sacred forest
into the cosmic, spiritual beings you really are. You are not what
you think you are and not what others think you are. You are you
and they are they. Different, unique, and wonderful in this inner
spirit. Your petty thoughts, feelings of fear, anger, jealousy, sadness are not real, but your loving, compassionate soul and spirit as
a child of God is. Open to the sacred and special wisdom and
understanding that we trees offer to you. And be whole and holy
before God so you can do the service in spirit as you are destined
to do.

(30) Acknowledge the forest and tree spirits and all the other
spirits of the forest and sky. Remember to bow—turning in a circle
three times—for you are part of the cosmos of divine and intelligent

order. Partake of its beauty, color, form, shape, and odor. We offer love through you and purpose to your feminine side for balancing with your masculine side. This transforms the ecological and spiritual from the secular so you can truly be who you are–a shining, loving star who loves life and extends protection to trees and forests as a special calling. Let petty thoughts and feelings flow away through changing. God heals through nature.

(31) Dead old log. We are rotting and useless logs to many human beings. Yet in reality, we are the very essence of the forest nutrition process. As we decompose, small microorganisms, fungi, and insects embrace us and help us to produce soil nutrients for all trees and plants. So we provide this service as a valuable part of the forest ecology picture of balance and impermanence of rising, existing, and falling away–not to mention our sponge effect of holding water in rainy season and releasing it gradually throughout the year. So we are not useless. We provide nutrients and water to life forms and forest cover. We are the final stages of change in trees, the natural process without interference from humans. We dead old logs are becoming the living essence of life itself.

(32) Mackay Tulip Oak. See my heavy clump staghorn ferns as they cling to one of my branches and build themselves up until they form a soft, heavy, leatherlike green mass, getting heavier and heavier until they finally come crashing down. Like many things that get heavier and heavier with life and attachments, they inevitably come crashing down with time. When greedy growth for its own sake comes, stop it before it gains a foothold in your mind.

(33) Mackay Tulip Oak. Why do most of you humans feel so good and peaceful like you are in nature? Then why do you humans develop and destroy the nature when you want and need it for survival and quality of life? Your primordial roots of hunting and gathering go back to the forest and call you back to your spiritual and ecological self in the forest. Yet you have reduced us

to small forest areas in your greed and cancerous growth of development. Heed the call while there is still time. Can you heed and protect the forest? See us in you and you in us in life and protect us.

(34) General rainforest. See that poisonous Eastern Brown snake dart under your left foot which you hold up through nature and instinct. You are attuned to the forest. You are in harmony with it. You are holistic and mindful. You have plugged in deeply to God and nature in instincts and intuition for living and working. Have gratitude for your life for God and his/her nature for giving you life and protecting you. Then know that you are a part of the forest and respond to it in love and trust for your soul.

(35) Mackay Tulip Oak with magnificent buttresses. Who and what created us? God, nature, accident, evolution, whatever. Behind everything is love. God is love. He/she gave order and intelligence to the universe or cosmos through love for creation of living forms. This love is reflected as my spiritual form, energy, bliss. This is me. Look at how magnificent and lovely we become as reflected in the trees now. You are at the dawn of love of trees, nature, and people, which makes you open and humble, open like humus. Love is all there is. It is all love.

I interact as a tree in the loving ecology of the rainforest. You are fortunate to be here and responding to the channeling. Write it up for a book. Show the love so it will do some good for God and nature and help to protect nature and trees and forests for present and future generations of all life.

(36) Leaf on forest floor. I am a leaf from a tree–fallen to the ground and dead, yet in process as I return nutrition and energy to the trees as I decompose. Many of my leaf friends feed the future of the forest as I do. We rise and fall away in different forms and are changed to our forest function of nourishment, humble but needed, divine in process, a simple leaf, but food and divine

breath for our trees. We are in the lap of the forest, dying or living. In dying, we live.

(37) Leaves in trees. Leaves—shades of green, levels of green, spaciousness of green, blending of green, flowing flavors of green—a glorious mosaic of green beauty and life. We leaves take the sun's energy and transform it for trees and plants. Great and humble we are abundant, common, and ubiquitous. Yet individual, unique and essential are we in the rainforest of life. Poised in energy and life as well as dying and dead on the forest floor, we are life. We are love. We are because we are. You existed just as you are. An ecological blend of brother and sister leaves, living and decomposing, opens to you and calls for protection of this green world which reflects God's cosmos of order and beauty.

(38) General rainforest along trail. The blue sky comes through the tree tops with the cosmos. Can you stand tall and notice this invisible connection which is ubiquitous for life and connected with mother earth like a bridge?

(39) Tree by Ranger cabin. Awareness. Are you aware of me and my brothers and sisters as we stand tall and beautiful around you? Can you sense an ecological and spiritual life essence as we connect with you? Be aware of us so that you are really a conscious part of planet earth and the cosmos—not that you are not, but many of you humans go through life without really being aware of us trees, let alone other living beings and nature. This is particularly true with your anthropocentric, materialistic, and mechanical views. Can you not see the trees for the forest or the forest for the trees?

(40) General rainforest along trail. Can you not realize that God created you, among other reasons, to have awe and to be aware of his/her creation? Too often, you shut us out or ignore us or are too busy or spaced out to see the beauty and spirituality of

the life-giving force of the trees around you. By ignorance, you, again and again, cut yourself off from the ecological awareness which makes us all one. And when you are cut off this way, you can do nothing of significance for yourself or for us.

Your energy and openness and love merely exist–almost dormant–when they could burst into wholeness with awareness. No one likes to be ignored or not acknowledged. And that is what you do to yourself when you are not aware and connected with yourself–the trees–the environment you are in. We come in different colors, forms, shapes, and spiritual essences that merge with you and come from you. Can you not feel it, seek it, enter it?

We beckon you to come to work–to come to us–for we are you and you are us and we love you. We do not want to be ignored or abandoned any more than you do. So come to us with your heart, mind, and body–physically, emotionally, spiritually, and mentally in nature for we like you are a manifestation of God. We have spiritual as well as ecological connections and consciousness with you. A bonding which asks that you protect us. And all this requires is your awareness–in love–in your heart.

(41) Red cedar. Look into me. Atonement is when you let go of ego and unwise ways which can cost trouble with me as well as with other ecology concerns, not to mention yourself. Let them go if they are in disharmony and discord with relationships and with tree work, so you can really be yourself. Release these boundaries, hangups, limitations by the ego, thoughts, feelings so you can get with the vibrations and sensations of the spiritual energy of impermanence of the living forest and its divine order of the cosmos. Just as I am–a red cedar, part of a forest ecosystem, living and dying, rising and falling.

In your being in time and space, join with the tonal atonement/alignment dance of life. Be who you are, not obligated or awkwardly trying to impress others, hurting yourself and nature. Be the natural you–this is how you can best serve your mission of protecting trees–by being free, by letting go of erroneous thinking and illusions. We want you to be free, to be unbound so you can really help us and be open in heart, mind, and body. Look at the leaves in rain. Like them, shake off and not retain all the guilt, anger, sadness, hangups in your past or the worry and depression of your future. The leaves beckon you as I do to be alive and attuned to the present moment in the life around you and protect the trees.

(42). General rainforest. We trees try to be good ancestors which is our greatest responsibility for future life. It depends on our returning to the earth and our evolution. Look at us. See the strength and love. See the support of other trees. We love you and always will. We are channels of God for you to get messages to serve because God loves you and heals you to do his will and wills you the strength, love, and courage to undertake what he wants and wills. So trust him and trust us to deliver his message. See our grounding in roots. Our evolutionary history as well as we reflect the cosmic universe that created us. Be with us for you are us and we are you and become one with all past, present, and future trees.

Your message is to plant seeds where appropriate, not scatter them inadequately or compulsively all over the place to gain acceptance. Be discerning and wise, otherwise you get hurt, for you are vulnerable and sensitive like we are and need to protect yourself or you will feel abandoned, hurt, and depressed through your ego and clinging instead of your good spirit. Be carefree in thought, word and action. Be attuned to God and trees so you can really be you and not what you think you are supposed to be or do in this life.

As a soul in this lifetime, you may be with or without a partner. You will be given one if she fits with the big picture and if she is good for you and you are good for her, each available to the other's growth. Otherwise, it is best that you remain alone and do your life without this partner relationship. Regardless, you do need to bring out your feminine side more into life as well as your masculine side so that they balance and subsume and are in harmony with each other for love and compassion, which will help you in understanding your life, the world, and spirituality.

Above all, be a good ancestor. You know not what happens after this life or what can happen in the future. But you do know that being a good ancestor is passing along the necessary and natural heritage with protection of trees and forests. We all want to be eternal, don't we? If there is any choice for your being eternal, particularly as a soul part of the spiritual essence of God, it is by your being a good ancestor and contribution to all life through your life and work with trees. This is the answer that you have been waiting for. This is your life; so use God, use yourself, and particularly use us trees to be there for you to help to gain your insight and wisdom. You need it.

Make conscious contact with us. Bring us into your life as much as you can for we are good for you. Your mind/ego is often out to get you with silly, stupid, and harmful thoughts and illusions with greed, anger, fear, darkness. You cannot fully and wholly participate in the present moment or do the service which is needed. Bring us into your life now so you merge more and more. For like yourself, we are living spiritual beings and our channels reflect God in all his glory, wisdom, love and power to you as a human being. And we love you and know that you love us, too, and will help us as much as you possibly can.

Remember that we are part of the community/ecology. But you cannot save the whole environment, so you need to keep this in mind in your approach. Your focus needs to be on trees and forests. Let others handle other aspects. Focus on us, for we are identified and loved by you. We need to dialogue more, but my brothers and sisters are giving a lot of messages now. They are urgent and well need to be published. Try to do it in a popular book so it can reach people and do some good for protecting forests and trees which cannot protect themselves.

So we call out to you and offer our love and compassion for help to get the message out so that something can be done. Much of this involves spirituality for change for reaching the heart as well as the minds of humans. For they cannot be good ancestors the way they are willfully and ignorantly permitting trees and forests and plants to be destroyed throughout the planet. They will be called cursed ancestors instead of good ones who consider protection of life to be crucial and unite against the destructive.

(43) So alone. You think you are so alone when you relate to trees. But you are not "so alone."

You are "so blessed." You are chosen to do this with an open heart. You are opened in this spiritual direction for your life. You must give up petty and silly thoughts and dire feelings that immobilize you and make you unhappy as you dwell on them. Silly little problems–let them free and not clinging in your space. You are too noble and natural, so just let go and tune to the present moment where you are; live life–just do it–not that negative stuff. Then you can be fully alive to the glory of God and be real, like a tree.

(44) Be different and accept it. You are not a dependent, approval-seeking being who must beg life from other human beings. You are different, as they are. You do not need to depend on them for their sad and silly approval. That makes you feel so abandoned, so worthless when there is no response or when they are unavailable. You have roots. Use your roots which help Mother Earth. Do not extend yourself beyond them only to be hurt.

Be yourself and enjoy being yourself. Let all differences and individual ways be. Celebrate your differences so that they can be in harmony with yourself and other beings. Count your blessing of individualization. Remember your truths. Remember your dignity. And protect yourself so you can protect us.

(45) Eagle Heights Retreat Center Rainforest. So you forgot your regular notebook. You are a child of God and loved like all his children. You make mistakes, errors, wrong choices. So what? What do you expect of a child with a limited vision of the infinite. Be

good to yourself—no condemnation. Be compassionate, be kind to yourself and other children of God. Be forgiving of yourself and others. See the golden green streaming through the trees. Your camera does not work. So what? There are other times and places. This is not the only time and place. In spirituality, time and place are meaningless anyway.

Do not condemn yourself while sitting with the golden green leaves nearby. You simply had to change to much different choices. You need to realize that you can choose. So choose again and again if necessary. Then you can really be who you are and not disturbed by your mental and emotional bodies. It is time to be your real self—your ecological self of relationships from and with your heart. We love you and we are glad to hear you say, "I love you too."

Be happy to be alone. If you are not happy alone and you do not love life, how can you really want us, except through love and happiness for all life and for us trees? Your mission is life. We love you and you love us—so let it be. Do not condemn yourself or others. Enjoy yourself and enjoy other beings. Remember that all are equal. We are all spiritual beings, living beings. No one is better or worse than anyone else. So be it.

(46) Rainforest. You must allow your feminine side to emerge more. Recognize and accept it and love it. When repressed, it makes you too needy and seeking of the feminine so you become immobilized and too fearful of rejection and change and try too hard to impress. Don't do this to yourself. Look at us trees. Many of us are both male and female. And we accept this. It is in balance. Do not make errors by consciously or unconsciously seeking needy stuff to bring this side into yourself. Just be natural and allow this feminine space and time to emerge and be comfortable and compatible and offer its depths, compassion, love, sex, and spirituality to you. Do not feel threatened by it. Just let it be outside and inside of you for what it is with love and do not cling.

Do you not see the need now to be a good ancestor? You are to pass this love and spirituality of trees and forests to other generations so all can be protected for life. But be attentive to your moods and intuition and vibrations. Yesterday, you could not get it right when you tried. Remember, we die eventually as our leaves die and pass to other trees and plants in nature through the recycling of our energy and molecules, but also of spirit, our essence. Yet we have the capabilities to reach other humans like you. Some time, you will also do the same with your ashes–you in your capacity as an ancestor of all life, not just the human species, but through the evolution of divine intelligence and the order of the cosmos or universe, reflected and revealed to you through trees.

Thus, you have the responsibility and obligation to be a good ancestor for all life. Do you understand the nobility and love of this necessary as well as great responsibility, to undertake it for God and trees as well as for yourself and your soul? You need to impress the love of trees and nature which you have to give on the visible and invisible life forms of the present as well as those of the future. In this way, you join in the spiritual essence of life.

(47) You are different–celebrate your differences–your variety and your diversity. Be kind if you distinguish your special blessings which set you apart from others, but at the same time be ordinary and filled with humility as any tree or plant in the rainforest. You *are* your uniqueness, as well as your ordinariness as a member of the living community with all of us as we rise, exist, and fall away to impermanence. It takes humility and spirituality to forget your past and your own importance, to know the humility and spirituality in others, for it is this that we have in common: all living beings are impermanent.

When you are into ego, you are apart, separate. When you are common and ordinary with all beings, without disillusions and condemnations, balance and harmony can be present, particularly if you balance your masculine and feminine parts. It is a stance that will place you as a living member of our living ecology–our evolving community of life and the forest–not greater, better, or worse than any other member. Please honor this and really be yourself in equilibrium and equanimous with the living forest as a member and helper.

We love you for your honesty and love and for your just being you. God bless you this day in your combined diversity and dignity and for being the real you. It is great sport to be around you, your spirit and your essence. God brings you here. You are welcome and holy.

(48) Why be afraid of undulating and compulsive fear and helplessness? We are all conditioned but you do not have to fulfill your blood patterns. Don't be muddled in your thinking and participation—be wise and analyze. Don't talk carelessly and compulsively. Do not let your neediness rob you. Look at the forest in spiritual and ecological ways and patterns or ask us individually. We love you and you know it.

(49) Large eucalyptus tree in rainforest. I am divine. All living beings reflect the divine and the intelligence and order and universe through God. Your mission is trees but remember always the holy and deep ecology and spirituality of deep questions on which is happiness and survival of the fittest in community. Be glad I have chosen you. I speak in the spirit which gives you wisdom, understanding, love, compassion, and holy messages to change and heal yourself to protect the trees for present and future generations.

Fear not that you have a lot of fear, ambiguity, anger, and sadness. You are programmed with wisdom to overcome this conditioning. You are bigger than this conditioning. You have your spirituality and humility working for you. Change things to work for your advantage while letting go of control. Apply yourself to reality and it will work. Leave out the B.S.–no lies. Be honest and accepting of reality as you proceed with dignity for the good of the trees and yourself.

(50) Unchite tree in rainforest. Quit seeking to be understood and to understand everything. Do not expect to understand any human. You do not even understand yourself. You can act for change but do not ask to be understood by others. You are constantly changing anyway from moment to moment—so just accept that you will change. Stop trying to make things right and acceptable to people, or to get them to like you. Just be yourself. You are here to protect the trees.

CHAPTER FOUR

NORWAY, MONTANA, AND CANADA

(1) Tree on University of Oslo campus (August, 1990). Be aware/alert. Listen or you miss out, particularly with an agenda, projections, and expectations. Keep open. Do not judge. Be neutral for openness and diversity without illusions and delusions.

(2) Use your internal and intuitive compass. Make it simple and natural and listen to it.

(3) The dumbness needs to stop here. Take responsibility and risk—slow down and feel well formed energy with your arm (on tree)–life and spirit.

(4) Trees in Norwegian National Park. You forgot to pay attention to us and to listen to our messages.

MONTANA:

MYRTLE THE MAPLE (tree outside my apartment, Billings, Montana, 1990).

(5) Just hang out with those people who like and appreciate you. Stop trying to get everyone to like you or approve of you.

(6) Stand and sit tall and straight like me.

(7) You are a connecting bridge and channel between heaven and earth—between Father Sky and Mother Earth.

(8) Believe in life—be alive in the moment. You can only really connect with God and nature in the present moment.

(9) Hold me. Feel life and energy pulsating in me from the depths of the earth. It is given to you for centering and growth.

(10) You are worthy. Look inside, not outside, for approval.

(11) Feel the love and healing energy flow through us as you hold me. Stay alive, be happy.

HOLY HOLLOW (Forest of lodgepole pine, Engelmann spruce, alders, and quaking aspen on tribal lands above Yellow Bay of Flathead Lake, Montana, September, 1997).

(12) We are all different as individuals. So listen to us. Stop talking or projecting what we say on us. Just listen. Some of us may wish to talk. Some just a little. Some may not. Respect this. Do not interfere with our privacy or dignity.

(13) God is here. Everywhere and everything. A flowing love energy.

(14) Stay open and expectant. Do not flood the scene with expectations and self talk. Be in the void.

(15) Keep open. We reach out to you in love. Remember your mission and let negative thoughts go. Like impermanence. Let positive thoughts through. Keep your mind open for non-thinking. Be yourself, your natural self. Stop looking without. Stop thinking like a fool. And be yourself. We love you.

(16) Green, green grow we trees in our green habitat. Shades of green, columns of green, life forms of green. God bless green and its immense beauty.

(17) Are you not happy with me, Daniel? You have been with

me and will be with me always. Then be aware. I want you to be happy. Be happy. I love you. You are healed to serve and love.

FOREST TRAIL TO HIDDEN FALLS, MONTANA (summer, 1999)

(18) The forest teems with life–we trees burst with life. Be alive. Be aware. Feel the strong inputs of living trees. We urge you to be happy, be aware.

(19) Hemlock. Take my branch hand with its new, soft needles. Claim your right to be alone in the present moment. Let go the hollow illusions. Be happy. Be here.

(20) Look at the diversity: the mountain ash, the hemlock, the aspen, the moss, thimbleberry bushes and other life. All have their individual needs–all are different–yet all are the same in Oneness and life. Respect these differences whether it be the lofty ponderosa pine or the tiny hemlock seedling below it. Do not judge or compare any living being with another, including yourself.

(21) See the captivating life of the forest. We trees with shades and forms of green plead with you to be aware. Be with us–the beauty, the spirit of the forest, the color, all of us. Be aware.

HOLY HOLLOW Montana (July, 2000)

(22) Tamarack tree. Yes, you can touch me lightly. Feel the powerful energy from my trunk to you and connect with the earth. It is powerful and spiritual and limitless for connection with Oneness. Feel free. See the scar on my trunk. I am healing myself, just as you must, so we can both be part of the beautiful nature of life. Be happy.

(23) Quaking aspen. Be patient and wait for healing for life for your mission. Trust God and yourself. Save the trees yes—but be patient in doing this. You will do it, whatever your tree mission. Be yourself. Trust.

(24) Mountain maple. I am bright and bushy and part of the understory. I belong and so do you. We are living beings in nature. Earth, me, and you in this moment. Be happy.

CANADA

TREE CHANNELED POEMS (Forest Camp, University of British Columbia, August, 2000)

The tree is me
And I am that tree
A tree of male, female, or gender both that tree and me are in the same boat
For we are in Oneness
And merge with the other's living beingness to open to energy and life while that tree bridges the cosmos without strife.
Sunlight through the trees
Dark shadows on all of us
Can light be dark?
Can dark be light?
Can light be dark?
And dark be light?
Yes, says the Dhamma nature
Of emptiness and formlessness
For impermanence changes all, nevertheless.

Tropical forest, Northern Queensland, Australia

Tropical forest, Northern Queensland, Australia

Tropical forest stream, Mount Tamborie National Park,
Southern Queensland, Australia

Fern palm, Eagle Heights Retreat Centre, Queensland,
Australia

Umbrella palm, Eagle Heights Retreat Centre, Mount
Tamborie, Queensland, Australia

Author with large tree buttress, Euglena National Park,
Queensland, Australia

Twin tropical trees, Euglena National Park, Queensland, Australia

Old growth tropical tree, Euglena National Park,
Queensland, Australia

Author by tropical tree with nodule, Mount Tamborie
National Park, Queensland, Australia

Tropical forest canopy, Euglena National Park,
Queensland, Australia

Strangler fig tree encompassing its host tree, Euglena
National Park, Queensland, Australia

Tropical forest scene, Mount Tamborie, Queensland,
Australia

Tropical tree at Pitak Court, Bangkok (while still alive)

Ajahn Maha Gosandra (first from right in front row)
leading Buddhist Monks in march at forest protection
meeting, Cambodia

Buddhist Monk in tropical forest in Taplan National Park,
Thailand

Holy hollow forest walk, tribal lands, Yellow Bay,
Montana

Author on Hidden Falls trail, Ronan, Montana

"Myrtle the Maple" at back of apartments, Billings,
Montana

Forest meadow in national forest, Montana

Old growth Engelmann Spruce in national forest,
Montana

PART TWO
TREE TALES

After a guided tree meditation, tree tales will involve stories, legends, and myths about trees and forests from "A Tree's Plea," "A Tree Grows in Bangkok," Buddha and Asia, Nepal, the Celtic countries, and Finland. In many ways, these tales speak to the heart and bring out their own messages for personal and Deep Ecology change.

GUIDED TREE MEDITATION

Slowly take five deep breaths: (1) mindfully breathing in, mindfully breathing out, (2) mindfully breathing in, mindfully out, (3) mindfully breathing in, mindfully breathing out, (4) mindfully breathing in, mindfully breathing out, (5) mindfully breathing in, mindfully breathing out.

Now feel the soles of your feet as they contact Mother Earth. Feel the bottom of your feet as roots slowly start to emerge from them. Feel your roots going deeper and deeper into Mother Earth—deeper and deeper, deeper and deeper, deeper and deeper. Feel how your roots are firmly anchoring you and grounding you to Mother Earth.

Now root branches gradually start to emerge from your tree roots. Your root branches, in turn, develop root hairs that are able to absorb the liquid nutrients provided by soil from Mother Earth through osmosis, a process that allows liquids to pass through the semi-permeable cell walls of the root hairs. This process permits the nourishment of Mother Earth to enter your tree root system through soil nutrients.

As the soil nutrients with their liquid nourishment enter your tree root system, they begin their upward journey through phloem vessels of the outer living cambium layer of the tree trunk, the narrow layer between your tree bark and its inner core of wood cells. The nourishing liquids from Mother Earth continue their journey up your tree trunk until they reach the tree branches and leaf stems; they finally reach your green leaves.

Your leaves contain little green factories of chlorophyll. As the sun power of Father Sky falls on the leaves and their green factories with their nutrients/nourishment from Mother Earth, a miracle of life and energy takes place. Photosynthesis, combining the nourishment from Mother Earth with the sun power of Father Sky through chlorophyll in the leaves, produces raw liquid energy. This energy is transported and used by every living cell in your tree body from your deepest root to the tip of your tree crown.

Notice the small black openings on your leaves. These openings are called stomata that are breathing openings. As a tree, you inhale carbon dioxide that is exhaled from other living beings. In turn, you exhale oxygen that is inhaled by other living beings in the animal world. So you are exchanging the breath of life in a Oneness of interrelationships and interdependencies with other beings in that they need your oxygen just as much as you need their carbon dioxide.

It is recognized that molecules of oxygen have never left the living earth since its beginning. Hence it is possible that one of the oxygen molecules that you are exhaling for other living beings might have been inhaled by Buddha over 2,500 years ago when he became enlightened under a tree.

Now look at your leaves. Some of them are young, some are middle aged, and some are old and dying and about to fall to the forest floor. This is the process of impermanence of rising and falling away, of rising, existing, and dying which all living organisms must do. When the old and dying leaves fall, insects and microorganisms will break down their materials and turn them into soil nutrients which, in turn, will be used by Mother Earth as nourishment for you and other trees.

Over the years, impermanence will also cause you to eventually die and fall to the forest floor where, you, too, will, like your leaves, have insects and microorganisms turn you into soil nutrients as you become part of the ecological processes of nature in the living web of life.

Look at your tree body of trunk, branches, and leaves. Notice all the living beings that have made your body their home or habitat for feeding, mating, nesting, and shelter. Notice the bird life and the animal life and the insects that call you their living home or habitat.

You have interactions, interdependencies, and interrelations with these creatures as well as with the forest ecosystem as a part of the living web of life. You communicate with your fellow trees as part of your forest community and neighborhood. Feel the energy and connectedness of this Oneness with all the living things in your forest home. Feel like it is to be a living tree in a forest.

But as a tree you are vulnerable. You are anchored to Mother Earth. You cannot run away when danger or the logger comes to cut you down. Yet you are noble and spiritual as a living tree being. You are a spiritual bridge between Mother Earth and Father Sky from the very endings of your roots to the top of your tree crown.

Feel this connectedness within yourself and without in your surrounding ecology. Feel the energy and vibrations of life going through you. Feel the nourishment from Mother Earth along with the sun power from Father Sky as they combine in your leaves to produce energy which passes through your entire tree body.

You are a tree, a living, spiritual, and noble being of life and nature. Feel how it is to be an inseparable part of the wholeness of nature, of the web of life.

Feel like it is to be a tree.

Feel how it is to be a tree.

You are a tree.

And now we will slowly return to our human form as we deeply breathe five times as our tree branches return to our arms and our roots return to the soles of our feet.

(1) Mindfully breathing in, Mindfully breathing out, (2) Mindfully breathing in, Mindfully breathing out, (3) Mindfully breathing in, Mindfully breathing out, (4)Mindfully breathing in, Mindfully breathing out, (5) Mindfully breathing in, Mindfully breathing out.

You have now returned to your human form. But remember how it was to be a tree as a living, spiritual being.

May all beings be happy (End)

"Standing like a Tree" (tree song)
Standing like a tree with my roots dug down
My branches wide and open
Come down the rain
Come down the sun
Come down the fruits to the heart that is open to be. . . .
(repeat)

A TREE'S PLEA

While a Senior Fulbright Research Scholar in South East Asia, the four park guards and I climbed a steep hillside in the tropical forest in Tublan National Park, Thailand. Suddenly, we came upon a magnificent tree–huge and noble. It would take three men to get their arms around it. I estimated it to be over 400 years old and 120 feet in height. A few simple branches at the top of the huge trunk seemed to reach into the heavens. There were relatively few leaves on the branches, but the top of the tree was like an open hand reaching outward. It was powerful, gorgeous, and natural.

I put my hands on the trunk of the tree and felt captured by its energy. It was like holding another human being. I felt powerful but calm, with a balanced and harmonious energy that seemed like the essence of life itself. I felt the energy flow from the very womb of the earth to reach through the trunk and its open branches to embrace the sun and the sky. The energy seemed to be flowing both ways between God and the Earth with light and love.

I held onto to the tree and was spellbound. The park guards stood watching me as I pretended to be studying the tree scientifically. But I was experiencing one of God's creations. Then I heard (or thought I heard) an appeal emerging from the tree and its energy. It simply said, "Protect me."

Tropical forests are rapidly disappearing at approximately 100 acres a minute on a global basis. Many experts believe that tropical rainforest areas will be mostly deforested in Asia and elsewhere by the early 21st century. Most scientists recognize that they will not regenerate in similar, complex forms. National Parks and other protected areas provide the only real means of survival for remaining rainforests. But the protection must be internal as well as external. Tropical forests are fragile, vulnerable and complex ecosystems with diverse and abundant life. Poaching of timber and wildlife can create serious abuses and inroads into the ecosystem and park integrity, particularly when dominant trees are removed.

When we finally started down the hillside, I felt a sense of tragedy, as if something was very wrong. We were going cross country down a steep slope. Then we came upon a magnificent tree, huge and beautiful like the other. But it was lying down. It had recently been cut down by log poachers. The tree was being cut with a hand saw into small beams to be carried out. The tree would bring about US$800 on the local market. It had been cut down in a watershed drainage area of the national park. A feeling of sadness surrounded the downed tree and the beams being taken from it–almost like a friend had died. I went over to the tree–touched and blessed it. (End)

A TREE GROWS IN BANGKOK

With its teeming millions, massive developments, skyscrapers, and traffic jams along with heavy air and loud noise pollution, Bangkok may not be the greatest habitat or environment for trees. Yet, somehow, this huge capital of Thailand still has a number of nice, old trees that grace this Asian city. These trees are often considered to be sacred and bestow blessings on many as they bring a touch of the nature and beauty of old Siam before the developed and industrialized Thailand. This is the story of one such tree that grew and died in Bangkok.

After World War Two, when there were plenty of trees, it is reported that officials from the U.S. Agency For International Development were disappointed with the laid back Buddhist Thais who were not consumer or development oriented. To remove this peaceful and contented Siamese and Buddhist attitude, these officials induced the government and some Buddhist monks to "educate" the populace to be greedy consumers and developers so that they would be a good market for American goods. And, with this change of attitude, many, many old trees, along with Siamese traditional homes, were lost as development forced its way everywhere in the big city and countryside.

Several years ago, I was a Fulbright Scholar studying tropical forests in Thailand. I decided to rent an inexpensive, one room flat in Bangkok as a base camp for my travels to national parks and wildlife sanctuaries. I finally found one at Pitak Court and still use it today while spending winters in Asia for environmental consulting and summers in Montana.

What made me immediately take the flat was a beautiful, large tropical tree right outside the window of the flat. After chugging up four flights of stairs, I entered the flat and looked out the window to find myself in a single canopy or crown of a magnificent and beautiful tree that seemed to instantly connect with me and I with it. It gave me the impression of being healthy, holy, and wise–even happy.

I estimated the tree to be slightly under 100 years old. It was majestic and gave me an impression of Oneness with the surrounding pond and old Siamese estate that bordered Pitak Court. The city's outline of skyscrapers and massive developments along with heavy air pollution failed to diminish the noble and healthy stance that I started to simply call Tropical Tree.

At heart and in appearance, it was a wild tropical forest tree and not a domesticated one like those planted around developments. I preferred to call it by the generic and symbolic name of Tropical Tree so it could represent the hundreds of tropical forest tree species worldwide. Moreover, naming or classifying a species scientifically often implies control and I did not wish to control this wild, free, and beautiful tree.

Tropical Tree had grown next to an old fence separating the Siamese estate, with its classic and traditional home, from Pitak Court. Its tree trunk was straight with branches radiating at upward angles as if it were enfolding arms to embrace the cosmos. All different stages of leaf growth were present with the bright green of young leaves, middle aged green leaves with less color, and the older leaves, losing their color and about to fall to the ground.

These stages reflected the classic Buddhist concept of impermanence where everything is rising, existing, and falling away.

Everything is constantly changing. With time, I would notice that a group of young, bright, green leaves had become larger and less colorful. Then they would get older and their green color would fade. In the same manner, I would notice the sudden emergence and disappearance of small, beautiful and colorful tree flowers.

Right beside Tropical Tree was an additional bonus: a large old square pond. All sorts of aquatic life were contained in the brown, murky, and fertile waters of the old pond, including fish, a long and mysterious stick-like fish that would surface occasionally, and numerous small and two huge ones.

When an old lady from the Siamese estate would throw cabbage leaves on the pond water, the surface would literally explode with teeming, aquatic life. If lucky, from my perch in the flat, I would get to see one of the mysterious stick-like fish or a huge turtle. It was like looking down from the canopy of a forest tree which it actually was. Between Tropical Tree and the pond, I had a wonderful presence of nature, ecology, and life–perfect for an ex-park ranger naturalist like myself.

My real interest was in Tropical Tree who was constantly beside me and became a companion. I felt like I was living within its bountiful canopy. Besides its beautiful flowers and new leaves, it was always surprising me with some form of life appearing or reappearing in its canopy like a colorful bird or butterfly, an insect or a leaping squirrel.

I did a certain amount of writing with my computer on a table facing Tropical Tree. I would constantly glance up at its canopy to see what forms of life were coming or going as an observing window naturalist. Yet, simply looking at my Tropical Tree was all I needed to connect with nature and the spirit of this wonderful tree that I had grown to love over the years.

My observations helped me to learn about as well as admire the small creatures that visited the canopy. I had always assumed that the holes in some of the leaves were the result of insects. Then I observed birds pecking and feeding upon some of the leaves so that small holes started to appear, particularly in the younger leaves.

I was dazzled by the numerous and colorful bird species and how they would all fit into their respective ecological niches. They were living examples of diversity, order, and cooperation.

I was amazed at the agility of small squirrels with large, furry ears. They would leap incredible distances from branch to branch in the canopy and then be off to run along telephone lines and fences. Colorful and captivating butterflies would appear, disappear, and then appear again as they flew and nestled in the canopy habitat of Tropical Tree. They and the other forms of life seemed to be just right and welcome in the ecology and surroundings of the canopy.

When the various life forms in the canopy and the pond had temporarily quieted down, I would simply look at Tropical Tree and admire its beauty, tranquility, and living form. It seemed to connect me with nature and to reassure me that all was well in that we were both living beings on planet earth and grounded.

It was a wonderful tree. I felt spiritually, emotionally, physically, and mentally connected to it—even if I was not aware of this connection at times. When discouraged, lonely, or depressed, it gave me hidden and silent messages, which were to hang in there, to trust God and myself, to know that this, too, would pass, to remember that I was a part of nature, to remember my life mission to protect trees like it, to be with the reality of life and not illusion, and other important advice. I know that I would have saved myself a lot of grief and pain by paying more attention to these messages and applying them.

I loved Tropical Tree. It was my friend and I was always in close proximity to it when in Bangkok. During the good and the bad times while working as a UN environmental consultant in Asia, Tropical Tree was there. Its presence would welcome me home and bid me farewell when I left. It would often surprise me with the sudden appearance of a colorful bird or butterfly, a leaping squirrel, or tree flowers in its canopy at eye level from my window.

I would try to meditate early every morning for an hour in a chair by the window. During and after my meditation, I could feel the presence of Tropical Tree stronger then ever with its calming, natural and deep spiritual influence. It is no wonder that Buddha selected a tree to become enlightened. Could it be that a tree, representing nature or Dhamma, was necessary for Buddha to become enlightened?

More than 2,500 years ago, Gauthama Buddha was born in a forest. As a youth he meditated under Jambo trees, studied among the Banyan trees, and found enlightenment beneath a great Boddhi tree. A denizen of the forests for the next 45 years, he died beneath a pair of Sal trees among his disciples. The Buddha chose to live in the forest in order to imitate what he saw. He emphasized the value of living in the forest to his disciples and called on newly ordained monks to sit at the foot of a tree. Trees may have a lot more spiritual influence and wisdom than we give them credit for.

One morning while meditating, I heard commotion below. Looking down from my canopy window, I saw some workers draining the old pond and putting up a brick wall with tiles. The turtles and the fish in the pond were being exposed as the water level went down. I had a realistic hunch that they would end up as meals for the workers. I particularly worried over the long stick-like fish in that it might be an undiscovered species. I know that I had never seen anything like it before and an ichthyologist friend was intrigued when I described it to him.

After all, we have only classified 1.5 million species of plants and animals on planet earth. Leading scientists estimate that we may have as many as 10 to 100 million species yet to be discovered. And most of these undiscovered species are in tropical forests that are being destroyed at over 100 acres a minute so that only small patches of protected areas will be around in less than 20 years.

If the long stick-like fish is an undiscovered species, it may well join the approximately 250 species that are becoming extinct every day. There really was not that much flesh on its long, thin form, but enough to cook and eat. Someone would soon echo the Mexican truck driver who shot and ate one of the last two giant ivory woodpeckers with the words: "it really was delicious meat."

When I looked over the old Siamese estate later, I noticed numerous workers putting in brick sidewalks, building an ugly pavilion and a cement fountain, landscaping the grounds with domestic trees and bushes, and modernizing the old Thai House. Tropical Tree and I seemed to bond together as we both watched the ripping up of our familiar and old environment. The vegetation of the old Siamese estate had a wild and natural look with its random bushes and small trees that blended into the place. With modern landscaping, All of these had to be destroyed. We shared a feeling of sadness and loss as we watched progress take hold of the old place and the pond.

Then I recalled that someone had said something about a rich Thai man who had bought the old place. He obviously had plenty of money for modernizing and developing the old estate according to his urban tastes. So the workmen, materials, equipment, and new domestic plant and tree life descended. The traditional estate took on a new, unnatural, and manicured look which took the heart, natural spirit and beauty out of the place. Small domestic trees were planted in rows with their tops trimmed so they would bush out "properly." I sensed that Tropical Tree had compassion for these poor tame trees that could not grow as nature intended.

A particularly sad part was the artificial look of the old pond as viewed by Tropical Tree and myself from the canopy. The pond now had expensive gaudy looking tile work enclosing the clear water with a neatly trimmed dwarf hedge surrounding it and no living creatures within. In the middle of this new pool was a awkward-looking pipe system that let out small fountains of water when turned on. The new pond was ugly and dead.

So Tropical Tree and I were witnesses to a microcosm of modern development in Bangkok. Like the our oasis type one by Pitak Court, old Siamese estates, along with their old trees, were being transformed into modern and lifeless concrete with artificial greenery. Still, I thought Tropical Tree to be safe because it provided shade, natural beauty, and spirit to the area from its isolated place by the fence.

I only saw the new owner two or three times as he came out to inspect his newly developed estate. He looked too tense and hurried to relax and enjoy his manicured creation. On those occasions, I looked at Tropical Tree and shook my head. I could feel it doing the same.

As usual, I left Bangkok and Asia for a summer in Montana in April. When I returned to my Bangkok flat on a late October evening, I felt that something was very strange. But I was so tired from the long flight that I immediately went to sleep. When I woke up with the rising sun, I looked out to see Tropical Tree.

At first, I could not believe it. Tropical Tree with its marvelous canopy had vanished.

Then I looked down and saw a small, brick structure where my Tropical Tree had had its trunk and roots. It had been cut and killed so a strange little brick structure could use the space. It had been too natural and wise for the controlled order now in demand. Somehow, the new owner had determined that Tropical Tree simply did not fit with the general tempo of his controlled and developed environment. After all, Tropical Tree was wild, appearing as a natural tropical forest tree species that departed from the domestic scene now in view.

I miss my old Tropical Tree as I look out of my window. I miss its canopy with the myriad of birds, butterflies, and squirrels, its tree flowers and the different shades and shapes of its green leaves. Yet, the spirit of my missing Tropical Tree and the life in its canopy still seems to be around at times, to remind me to persevere in my work to protect trees.

I miss the friendship that I had with this wonderful, wise, and sensitive tree over the years. And how it supported and comforted me by just being there. I feel that I have lost a noble friend who was solid and stable–although certainly vulnerable to saw or ax.

And now when I look out of my window and see the blank space of its missing canopy, I partake of the skyscrapers, infrastructure, and heavy air pollution of Bangkok instead of the nature that I was offered by and through Tropical Tree. Sometimes, I wonder why I did not appreciate Tropical Tree more when it was alive and when it reached out to me in light and love.

Biologically, it is recognized that every organism is an individual and unique and different from similar ones. As an individual, my Tropical Tree was more than a unique individual to me. It was a friend who came into my life as a blessing in my efforts to protect tropical forests. In this sense, Tropical Tree had an unusual and spiritual personality that reached my heart and life.

Like my Tropical Tree, tropical forests, with their rich biodiversity, will be destroyed in the next 20 years with only small pockets of protected areas remaining. And these small pockets of "protected areas" (mainly national parks and wildlife sanctuaries) are being severely degraded by illegal logging, poaching, and encroachments. A great deal of this destruction is irreversible because the complex interactions of the biodiversity in tropical forests once destroyed cannot regenerate. The inter-connectivity had to arise together and cannot be recreated. Tropical forests, consequently, will not regenerate in their ecological complexities and biodiversity of different species with their complex interactions.

Much of the hope for the future of tropical forests everywhere depends on gaining political, public, and local support (including surrounding areas and/or buffer zones) for protected areas and for their establishment and preservation before it is too late. Some claim that the real hope may lie in strong and dramatic changes in societal values and areas through Deep Ecology and Spirituality. Internationally, nationally, and locally, current efforts in all spheres are having very little success with the continued destruction, deforestation, and degradation of tropical forests outside or in protected areas.

According to recent photographic research and demonstrated experiments, it is possible to photograph the actual imprint or outline of a plant or tree leaf even after it has been removed. Perhaps the uncanny spiritual outline of Tropical Tree and its canopy is still outside my window. There, Tropical Tree still offers me the help and support of its presence as I open more to it for my work in protecting trees. Perhaps the Tropical Tree that grew and died in Bangkok did not die spiritually. I can sometimes feel its presence—even if I cannot see it.

TREE TALES OF BUDDHA
FROM ASIA

While studying Buddhism in Asia over the past dozen years, I noticed that there were a number of stories about Buddha and his relationship to trees and forests. I was impressed with how many Buddhist monks, nuns, and lay people were very concerned about the forest; they would often relate stories about Buddha, trees, and the forest to me. This was particularly true at the various Buddhist Forest Monasteries where I would sometimes stay on meditation retreats, including Wat Suan Mokkh in Thailand. Some of these stories relate to Deep Ecology and change and are presented here.

The following are tales are adapted from the above experiences, the Jataka Tales and from Professor Chaetsumarm Kabilsvak who is the chairman of the Education Committee of the World Fellowship of Buddhism, Bangkok, Thailand.

(1) "A DOVE IN THE FOREST," (ADAPTED FROM THE JATAKA TALES IN WHICH BUDDHA WOULD OFTEN TAKE THE FORM OF AN ANIMAL IN HIS PAST LIVES):

A long time ago, there was a thick forest. Trees were fresh and deep. The air was crystal clear. It was sending echoes of birds singing a beautiful melody, enchanting comfortable life there. The sky was so blue and open. The forest was full of grace, hope and peace. In this forest, there were thousands and thousands of creatures living together as one in harmony with nature.

One day, a dove flew out of the forest to look for food for its babies. When she returned, the dove saw a big fire rising up in the forest! All the living creatures, including birds, animals, plants, and flowers were trying to escape, desperately crying for help in this terrible disaster.

The dove was astonished to see this happening, yet had no time to think. She immediately flew off to a lake far away. When the dove arrived at the lake, she jumped into the water and had its body completely soaked. The dove flew up again and hurried to the burning forest. Flying back to where the fire was blazing briskly, the dove shook its body and dropped a few portions of water. Then she took off on a long flight to get to the lake again. In this way, the dove made many trips between the lake and the forest.

The Heaven, upon watching what was happening in the forest on the earth, asked the dove,

"Do you think that you of humble little body can cease the fire with those few shakes of water?"

The dove answered,

"The fire must be ceased as soon as possible. There are my children. There are my fellow creatures. And there is the very forest who nurtures all our lives. Everything is caught in a big fire now. I have to do something. I will continue making trips this way, until I die."

Eventually, the earnest wish and the prayer of this one little dove was taken to the Heaven. A heavy rain was brought to the forest and the fire was ceased. The forest returned to the peaceful, beautiful place that it once was.

(2)"THE BUDDHIST COMMUNITY AND FOREST DWELLING:"

The early Buddhist community was primarily comprised of forest dwellers so the members had to be mindful of the protection of the forest that was their basic abode. In every aspect, a community member had to respect each tree with which they came into contact.

A famous story tells how a Buddhist monk, while making repairs on his place, cut down a tree that was the abode of a deva. Although the deva urged him not to cut the tree, "to make an abode for yourself," the monk went ahead anyway. In doing so, he struck and cut off the arm of the deva's son, who was part of the tree.

When the deva reported this incident to the Buddha, he laid down a rule that forbade community members to destroy any living plant or tree. The story of the deva serves to help people understand that cutting down a tree is a selfish act. It disturbs the peace of others and deprives birds and wildlife of their natural habitat. It is also considered an ungrateful act since monks depend upon trees in their forest dwelling.

(3) "THE FIRST PRECEPT"

Most Buddhists know that the first precept forbids the taking of life. But very few of them may understand that the fundamental concept underlying this concept. This precept, taken literally at its face value, requires the negation of a specific action, namely killing.

However, to really observe this precept naturally and sincerely, one must not only refrain from a particular negative action, but also with intentions. One must be positive in his or her conduct as well. In this sense, the positive action is to protect and preserve living beings, including trees, which involves metta or loving-kindness.

Loving-kindness is based on denial of the ego that is the heart of Buddhism. When a person stops differentiating between themselves and other living beings and recognizes the Oneness of all living being, the practice of loving-kindness will flow without boundaries or limits. This is the true meaning of the First Precept or "Thou shalt not kill."

When loving-kindness is generated, people will extend their field of action to others. This brings about peaceful co-existence, not only to human beings, but to all living beings, including trees.

(4) "CONSERVATION OF LIVES"

Buddha and Buddhism respects and cherishes life in all living forms. Among many of the Buddha's teachings, one of his teachings is:

"He is one who abstains from injury to seed-life and plant-life. . . . Abandoning the taint of ill-will; with heart free from ill-will he abides having regard for the welfare and feeling compassion for every living thing; he cleanses his heart of the taint of ill-will."

(5) "BUDDHIST MONKS AND CONSERVATION"

The Buddha's disciples who were ordained as monks to follow the way to salvation are fully responsible for the protection of nature as witnessed by a system of forest monasteries in Theravada Buddhist countries in general and in Thailand in particular. Trees of all kinds enjoy protection in such monasteries along with birds and wildlife.

In many areas of deforested and degraded lands, forest monasteries provide an oasis of trees and nature. The monks often teach forest and wildlife protection to villagers as part of their efforts for the surrounding forests and protected areas. In numerous instances,

Buddhist monks have actually ordained trees as monks so that they might be protected. This ordination ceremony includes placing an orange robe around the tree.

(E) "THE BUDDHIST COMMUNITY AND THE FOREST"

The Buddha emphasized to his disciples the value of living in the forest for newly ordained monks. He called on them to sit at the foot of a tree. The Buddha said he chose to live in the forest in order to imitate what he saw (including impermanence of rising and falling away) and be helpful to those who came to him.

In the Rukka Suttra, the Buddha admired those who sat at the foot of trees, who desired seclusion, and who had few needs. These teachings encouraged his disciples to lead a forest life and prevent them from destroying the forest. The appreciation of nature by a Buddhist may signify his attempts to find a place of solitude, meditation, and seclusion to help with his/her practice and to attain liberation (Nibbana). It also constitutes one of the best methods for forest protection that has been offered to the world to bring out the sacredness and spirituality of the forest.

KATHMANDU, NEPAL TREE TALE

While doing a month long retreat at the Tibetan Kopan Buddhist Monastery on a mountain, I would look down at the Kathmandu valley in the early mornings to see a huge cloud of mist (and pollution) which appeared both mystical and captivating–like it was from another world. In the later morning, when the sun broke through, trees and buildings would gradually emerge throughout the valley cloud with a primeval and spiritual effect.

After the retreat, I met with a Nepalese scholar, Narayan P. Shrestha, who was the advisor to the King of Nepal, to ask him about this strange effect of the Kathmandu valley. He agreed with my impressions of his beloved valley and gave me some general and interesting information while referring me to his book. The following points are adapted and summarized from our conversation and from Narayan P. Shrestha, KATHMANDU THE ETERNAL KUMARI, Saros Kauz Lalitpur, Kathmandu, 1997):

At one time, the valley of Kathmandu, Nepal was a beautiful lake. It was surrounded by a magnificent herbarium with a diversity of trees in different shapes, sizes, and foliage due to different vegetation and altitude zones with abundant rainfall, ranging from subtropical and warm temperate to alpine, which all met in the valley. In those days, Kathmandu was recognized as an arboreal paradise with hundreds of species of trees along with numerous lichens, ferns and orchids.

Trees such as the cedar, oak, maple, hemlock, juniper, rhododendron, and Himalayan cherry were abundantly found in the mountains encircling the valley. Species like *Michelia champaca*, *Shorea robusta*, and *Pinus roxburghi* grew on the valley floor. In a literal as well as symbolic sense, the civilization of Kathmandu rested on its diverse, abundant, and unique trees.

This is why the quadrangular shrine of Kasthamandap, from which the city got its name, is said to made out of single tree, Michelia champaca. It was called "Kalpa Briksha" which means the "Heavenly Tree" that is capable of fulfilling everything one would wish for. In fact, the tree served as a metaphor for all wish fulfillment in life since it also signified the abundance of the arboreal kingdom that was once Kathmandu.

Like all great civilizations of antiquity, Kathmandu is also considered to be a river civilization with three major rivers. Along these river banks in little bushes lying under trees, there were a number of aniconic shrines which consisted of a few unhewn and uncut stones as nature had fashioned them. These shrines were worshiped as the Mother Goddess, Azima. In Sanskrit they were called Asta-Maatrikas which meant Eight Mother Goddesses. The early civilized inhabitants of India also worshiped a Mother Goddess.

This cult, in turn, had prevailed about the time that the sacred tree and fertility gods were also worshiped before 3,000 BC. in the Mediterranean and Middle East. With the exception of a few places in India, the cult of Mother Goddesses and trees, has disappeared from the rest of the world. Yet it has continued to be a living faith in the Kathmandu valley today.

With their faith in the esoteric Tantric cult, the ancient seers of Nepal believed that Azima was the Mother of the World. They considered her to be the consort of the first father who appeared at different times as Brahma the creator, as Vishnu the maintainer, and as Shiva the destroyer. In the Hindu sense, Azima needs to be understood as the motherly aspects of these primordial parents who divided into many forms and ways of distinct identities of Gods and Goddesses with various characteristics while still being One God and One God only.

In the beginning, Azima was One and One only, but the need arose to protect Kathmandu in eight cardinal directions. So, like a true mother wishing to protect her children, she assumed the roles of the Eight Mother Goddesses. These eight roles and forms with various identities and characteristics range from Kanya Kumri (Philbo Azima), a young virgin, to Indrayani (Luti Azima), a house-wife with her family as the cosmos, to Chamunda (Mhapi Azima), a goddess of death, to Mahaa Laxmi (Sri Azima), a nurturing and nourishing earth mother.

Azima, however, is really the eternal mother who embodies the female principle of the cosmos. Regardless of her different in-carnations or roles to display her varying traits, she is still consid-ered to be Mother Earth. She is the primeval womb that fecun-dates as the need arises. She is the primeval Mother who remains mysterious and elusive as the "eternal feminine." The past, present, and future all merge into her.

This goddess of compassion continues to take care of every living thing in the universe. At her command, the trees grow, the fields grow green, the birds sing, and wild flowers blossom. Azima or Mother Earth provides living, divine energy to all.

Her consort is Azu deo, the god of the sky, who sometimes descends into the earth to fertilize it with the rains to bring forth the trees, plants, and animals with Azima. Through the union of the father sky god, Azu deo, and the primeval mother earth god-dess, Azima, the curtain of life opens for all life in the universe, including the trees of Kathmandu, a valley and city, which is un-der the care of these two patron deities.

CELTIC TREE TALES

While visiting Findhorn, a spiritual community in Scotland a number of years ago, I learned about the Celtic and Druids (Celtic forest priests) stories and legends which usually involved trees from various Celtic countries. I was fascinated with the relationship of the Celtic religion and trees and have listed some of the common trees and their legends and related information.

Besides the above Findhorn visit, the following is summarized and adapted from CELTIC ASTROLOGY, Dynamo House, Melborne, Australia, n.d. and O.B. Conway, CELTIC MAGIC, Llewellyn, St. Paul, 1997:

The Celtic zodiac is based on the moon cycle with 13 months for the year. Each month is associated with a tree sacred to the Druids. According to the Druids, the human race originally was descended from the trees with each tree having unique magical qualities as well as detailed character analysis for 13 basic personality types. The following will focus only on magical or mystical qualities of selected, sacred Druid trees:

(a) ASH: This tree was considered to be a sacred chieftain tree. It was said "to court the flash" since it was prone to lightning strikes. Ash wood is believed to be enchanted and it was used for wands and spears. Carved with decorations, ash wands were considered to be good for healing and solar magic. Fresh ash leaves put under a pillow would stimulate psychic dreams.

(b) ALDER: Alder resists water and it was used for bridges, boats, and containers. It was considered a crime to cut down an alder since the angry tree spirit would burn down the houses of those involved.

(c) BIRCH: The Druids considered birch to represent renewal or rebirth because it was the first tree to leaf after winter. Also known as the "Lady of the Woods," love incense and messages were made from its bark to attract lovers.

(d) ELDER: The elder tree was considered to be sacred for Fairies. Druids believed that standing under an elder tree would help one see the "little people." Elder branches were hung above stables to protect the horses from evil spirits. It was considered unlucky to burn elder or to bring it indoors. The Druids used elder to bless as well as curse. Elder wands or music from elder flutes could be used to drive out evil spirits or negative thought forms.

(e) HAWTHORN: This tree was considered to be a symbol of psychic protection because of its sharp thorns. Fairy spirits were believe to live in hawthorn hedges which were planted round churches and homes as protective shields. Wands made of hawthorn had great power while its blossoms were highly erotic to men.

(f) HOLLY: Celtic chieftains crowned their successors with a holly wreath. Holly was believed to repel enemies and warriors carried wood cudgels made of holly. When planted by a home, holly repels negative thoughts sent against one. During the winter solstice, it was used decorating and considered sacred. A bag of leaves and berries from a holly tree will increase a man's ability to attract women.

(g) OAK: Considered the holy and sacred tree of the Druids, the oak symbolized truth and steadfast knowledge. Oak doors were believed to keep out evil. The oak was also considered to be the king of trees in a forest with magic wands being made from its wood. When gathered at night, oak acorns were noted as having the greatest fertility powers while burning oak leaves purified the atmosphere. Druids and priestesses would listen to the rustling oak leaves and wrens in oak trees for divinatory messages.

(h) WILLOW: The willow was considered related to the moon. According to Celtic myth, the universe was hatched from two crimson serpent eggs which were hidden in the boughs of the willow. Willow groves were considered to be very magical so priests, priestesses and all types of artisans would sit among the willow trees to gain eloquence, inspiration, skills, spirituality, and prophecies.

Willows are also considered to be wishing trees. One wishes by gaining their permission, by explaining one's desire, or by tying a selected willow shoot around one's wrist while explaining what one wants, and by returning and untying the knot to thank the willow when the wish is fulfilled. One should always remember to express gratitude to the willow tree and to leave it a gift. (end)

FINNISH TREE TALES

During a brief visit to Finland, I noticed a great deal of interest in the mystical and healing aspects of trees. One Finnish forest researcher showed me a carved device from a tree that was placed over one's head to get rid of negative thinking, depression, and even sinus colds. He also pointed out how Finnish foresters and woodsmen would lean against a tree to get energy and spirit just as American Indians did during strenuous activities with a war or hunting party.

While in Nepal, I related my interest in the mystical aspects of Finnish trees to Markosmos Leppanen (Helsinki). Markosmos wrote down some very interesting information for me at the Himalayan Buddhist Meditation Center and later mailed me more for use in this book. The following is adapted and summarized from Markosmos:

The Finnish word for Forest, *metsa*, originally meant a border line between our side and the beyond. The one who crossed a border went to the kingdom of the bear, to the kingdom of Tapio (the God of the forest), to the kingdom of all kinds of *Haltija* (the keeper) spirits. One had to pay respect to these forces in order to walk safely in the forest.

In the forest, low growing mutations (wide but not tall) of spruce trees were known as the table of Tapio or Tapionpoyta. They were a special place to put offerings for the forest. Also, people would hug and kiss the earth so that they were at the soil with their whole bodies to salute the forest. If one were disrespectful to the forest, one might come under the spell of the forest or Metsanpeitto. This would include being covered by the forest or having physical marks on the body such as forest nose manifested.

The forests are not only part of the poems and stories; it was also a part of the religion and/or spirituality in the Finnish mind and heart. Under the image of the Cross and the Ax, Christian priests and ministers made large efforts to cut out the holy or "pagan" trees and forests in the 13th-19th century. The Christian Church did not like the original Finnish "pagan" nature religion at all. It is my understanding that pagan means country dweller among other interpretations.

As an example of this attitude, Christianity changed the meaning of *Hiisi* which originally meant the same as *Uhrilehto* or a part of the forest which is a holy offering area. But the priests and ministers made *Hiisi* synonymous for the devil so the holy forest was turned to mean something completely evil, like Satan, in their interpretations.

At the end of the 19th century, some priests were still carrying out operations to cut down "pagan" trees under the original authority of the Pope. During WW II, in late 1944, Nazi German troops burned 90 percent of the buildings in Northern Finland and cut away many of the family "pagan" or *Kotopuni* (a holy offering tree usually in the yard of a home) trees as a kind of psychological terror to destroy the tradition and morale of the people.

During the 1960s, there was a great deal of rural to urban movement among the population with a decrease of tribal tree mysticism. In modern times, the tree traditions and legends were almost lost along with the logging and development of old Finnish forests and trees.

However, in the nineties, two Finnish photographer women,

Ritva Kovalainen and Sanni Seppo, photographed the holy trees in a beautiful picture book, *Puiden Kansa*. This book helped to revive the consciousness. of Finnish people for their forest and tree traditions and mysticism. As a result, many are now active in fighting to protect the trees, especially since logging and developments are serious threats to the remaining old-growth forests of Finland.

Thus the rich traditions, spirituality, and mysticism associated with Finnish trees and forests contributed to their protection and heritage today. For example:

The Finnish national epic, *Kalevala*, was collected from Karelia 150 years ago. Before that, it had been transmitted from generation to generation in a form of oral heritage. The unbroken heritage of *Kalevala*-masters, poem-singers, and "knowers" (or *Tietaja*) has continued from time immemorial.

Kalevala deeply illustrates a world where trees and other living species in nature have consciences and can talk to human beings. For example, in the 44th poem of *Kalevala*, a birch tree is telling the main shaman hero, Vainamoinen, how she is suffering when children are cutting her with knives, when bark or branches are torn from her, or when she sees men with axes. She is crying. Then Vainamoinen tells her not to complain or cry since she will soon cry in happiness in a new, better life. Vainamoinen then sacrifices the birch tree in order to make a magical *kantele* (traditional folk music instrument) out of her. When the *kantele* is ready, Vainamoinen plays it in the forest. Trees, flowers, birds, even worms, move and dance with joy. Hills and rocks are shaking in a cosmic celebration of consciousness to be in union with Mother Nature.

At the University of Helsinki, modern shaman Johannes Stala indicated that central European wood buyers are now demanding certificates that the wood is not logged from old primeval forests. But he added that, before commercial logging, certificates should also be required that the forest's spirit was released by a shaman and that all the necessary forgiveness rituals be done. Otherwise, he and other nature sensitive practitioners, including shaman Esko

Jalkanen, are saying that a forest violently logged without ritualistic preparations will leave its aura standing erect for a long time.

In early Finland, almost everything was made of wood. On the other hand, it was believed that every tree is a sentient soul or consciousness called *Haltija* which one should keep as a friend and not an enemy. So this dilemma of cutting down a tree by a logger involves knocking on the tree three times with the dull side of his ax. He would then inform the tree that he was sorry, but that he had to cut it down.

The result was that the *Haltija* moved out from the tree and the "spiritless" tree was then allowed to be cut without offense against the spiritual world or forest. The same method was used among the Lapplander. Sometimes, the lowest branch was supposed to be the place where the *Haltija* would go and it was removed before cutting the tree.

In Finnish folk songs and traditional stories, there are numerous references on how a tree or forest can be one's loyal friend and a compassionate listener when one is going through rough times. A tree can be seen as a psychotherapist who shares one's secrets and sorrows. A tree's silent response is based on acceptance of change of impermanence (spring brings leaves, summer ripens them, and fall takes them away). Many people go to the forest to get away from mental problems and the forest also acts as an anti-depressant.

Folk tradition also indicates that trees, in their compassion, can take away physical illness from people wherein the disease will later appear visible in the tree in some mutant form. In Estonia, couples with marriage problems get help when they were put inside a very old hollow trunk which is like a cave in a large, living tree. After spending a night together in the tree, fighting no longer existed. Tar comes from trees and there is a famous Finnish saying that, "if tar, sauna, and booze do not help, then the disease is lethal," and, "whatever you do, do it with tar."

The *Kotopuu* or holy tree grows in the yard of a home and it is normally an object of offerings. For example, the first milk of a human mother or cow as well as the first grains of the harvest and the first pieces of feast food are offered to the *Kotopuu*. Usually the fate of the family is believed to be connected with this particular tree.

The *Kotopuu* is planted or selected by the first members of the family who begin to live in a given place. It was said that it would be better if the tree selected were younger than the person who selects it. Otherwise, it may not be sure that the tree will start to cooperate and to protect the family.

It was taboo to break any branches off a *Kotopuu* or holy home tree. If such a violation happened, destruction or difficulties would come to the family. Newborn infants are brought to touch the tree. Then they were considered to be under the protection of the tree and the hidden forces behind it. As noted, Christian priests and ministers tried to destroy these holy family trees or *Kotopuu* because of their spiritual and mystical aspects.

Uhrileho was the name of a part of the forest that is considered holy rather than a single holy tree at a home like *Kotopuu*. The whole community would worship at the *Uhrilehto*. Many Christian churches were built on the site of *Uhrilehos* to stop these pagan rites and to bring Christianity in its place. But could the spirituality of these places also attract church sites?

WILDERNESS
SPRUCE

(1) THE SEEDLING

It was a spring day, and something was happening deep inside a sleeping spruce seed in a national forest of the Northern Rocky Mountains. It had been shed from the cone of an Engelmann spruce tree the previous fall and had been slightly covered with soil duff in a mountain meadow. Throughout the winter, the spruce seed had been lying dormant under the cold snow. With this spring day, the soil became warm and moist, and the embryo or baby spruce tree in the seed began to awake and grow. It was cradled by a rich, seed body or endosperm that was packed with starch, fat, and proteins. The juices in the seed gradually dissolved this food material to sugars and reformed proteins to feed the growing points of the embryo spruce.

Life began to flow in the baby tree that looked like a tiny ivory rod. There was a tuft of pale, needle leaves or cotyledon on one end of the rod. The other end of the rod was tapered and contained root cells. The ivory rod began to grow and develop as it used its liquid food from the endosperm.

As the spring continued, the spruce embryo grew fast and began to germinate. The seed shell became too small and gradually split open. The newly born tree or seedling emerged above the soil with its tuft of needle leaves beginning to grow straight up. Beneath the soil duff, its roots grew downward. The little tap root penetrated the ground and anchored the seedling. On the opposite end, the seed leaves had pulled themselves out of their endosperm and spread themselves above the seedling like the crown of a miniature palm tree. On the leaf tip of the little stem of the seedling, a terminal bud was tucked between the seed leaves; it would be the growing point of the spruce tree for its lifetime.

Besides the growing of needle leaves, tap root, and stem tip of the seedling, another important growing area was emerging inside the stem. The cambium layer, consisting of a single layer of cells, was starting to produce wood cells in the interior and bark cells on the exterior of the seedling's stem. This made the seedling grow in girth or width. The cambium layer would continue to do this by dividing its cells every spring and summer throughout the life of the tree. Each year, it would add an annual ring that consisted of light colored wood cells in the spring and dark colored wood cells at the end of the summer. The bark produced by the cambium layer continuously dropped or sloughed off with the dead wood cells accumulating. The cambium layer was really the only living, growing part of the seedling's stem.

As the rapid growing processes continued, the seedling was almost an inch tall by the first day of summer. It looked like a tiny palm tree with its spreading needle leaves. Life was flowing through it from the end of its tap root to the end of its needles. In fact, Spruce, the seedling, was simply bursting with the vitality and spirit of life on this fine summer morning, feeling a sense of community and Oneness with the surrounding plants and animals that were part of the web of life.

Surveying the surrounding back country, Spruce took in the majestic mountains, magnificent forests, and grassy parks that were home. Spruce felt fortunate growing up in a sunny open area in a small park or meadow of the forest, growing faster and stronger than some spruce seedlings who had landed in shady spots beneath other, larger trees. However, the other spruce seedlings were tolerant of shade like all spruce trees; many would eventually grow into big trees as they obtained or reached more sunlight.

Spruce felt a bit lonely in this meadow spot away from other trees. But there were plenty of other living things to talk to, and Spruce very much wanted to talk to the life nearby. In the green, grassy meadow where Spruce lived, a number of different kinds of wild flowers were growing in profusion. Pink fireweed, red Indian paintbrush, purple penstemon, white yarrow, blue harebells, yellow arnica and other wild flowers formed varied, colored patterns of vibrant life. The flowers seemed to be almost singing as they swayed softly and invitingly in the warm breeze of the mountain meadow.

Finally, Spruce called out to these wildflower neighbors with a shout, "Hello there! How are you flowers today?" There was a long silence.

Finally, a nearby yellow arnica replied, "Hello, tiny tree. We did not know you could talk. What's your name?"

Spruce looked up at the tall yellow flower cluster which was almost a foot higher than himself. The leaves on the stem of the arnica seemed to be waving a friendly greeting. The seedling responded, "Spruce, I guess, or at least that's what I've been calling myself. My relatives and I are called Engelmann spruce and we live in the higher parts of the Rocky Mountains. What's your name?"

The arnica replied, "Oh, just call me Herb. After all, I'm supposed to be some kind of a medical wonder. My relatives and I grow about anywhere–from the valleys to the mountains. But a lot of living things like yourself can only live in certain places like your tree family–way up in the mountains."

Spruce hurriedly said, "But I really like it up here. I'd rather be in this high mountain meadow than any other place in the world. But, say, what's this about your being some kind of medical wonder?"

Swaying back and forth proudly, Herb answered, "That's right. Some people use my leaves to stop bleeding from wounds and cuts. Indians also make a salve out of my leaves and use it to heal infections and to treat sore and aching backs, arms, and legs. A lot of plants like me are used for food or medicine. By the way, what are you used for? "

Spruce, replied, "Gee, I don't know. I'm just happy to be alive for its own sake without worrying about how I am going to be used by something. I guess I just want to be a living free spirit with all the rest of the life around here."

"That sounds pretty good to me, Spruce," Herb commented. "But I understand that people use trees like you–when you are a lot bigger of course–for lumber to make buildings, houses, and things. They cut trees down and. . . ." Herb suddenly stopped talking as a large mule deer doe drifted into the small meadow. The mule deer gazed about with her large eyes searching the area and the long, mule-like ears flopping about her antlerless head. The doe's black nose sniffed the wind. Finally, she turned and summoned two small fawns who were covered with white spots.

One of the fawns tried to nurse some milk from the doe, but she warded him off while beginning to browse. Gradually, she worked toward Spruce and Herb with the fawns dangling behind her. Plucking at the grasses and shrubs of the meadow, she decided that something unusual would be nice. Spotting Herb, she immediately began plucking away at the arnica. The doe frowned a bit because Herb had a somewhat bitter taste, but she persistently continued to eat until there seemed to be nothing left of the lone plant. Watching, Spruce was shocked and saddened that his new friend had disappeared. Spruce trembled with fear as one of the doe's hoofs came down very close, leaving a large imprint on the ground. Spruce would have been crushed to death if the hoof had been just to the right.

Unaware of the havoc she had caused, the mule deer turned around toward the mountains. Spruce could see her white rump patch and narrow black-tipped tail as she ambled toward the waiting fawns. Then, all three gradually merged into the surrounding forest as they drifted from the meadow.

Looking at the vacant spot where Herb had been, Spruce felt both sad and lucky. Spruce did not know that Herb was a perennial and would spring from his root next year. Spruce had witnessed a vital part of the struggle of life in this mountain, forest home with living things in their struggle for survival. Spruce reflected on how many other spruce seeds had become seedlings. Poor conditions would prevent some from growing large or even germinating. Others would be eaten by wildlife such as squirrels and birds. And still others would be trampled and crushed. Only a few ever get to be large spruce trees if they survived these and other dangers.

Spruce admired the large Engelmann spruce trees in the nearby forest. Their spire-like forms with deep blue-green color gave a majestic beauty to them. At breast height, their trunks were up to a yard in diameter and covered with russet red bark that was broken into thick, loosely attached, small scales. Several were well over 100 feet high and hundreds of years old. Spruce often wondered which one had produced the cone containing Spruce's seed. But the large trees appeared too far off and too big to talk to. Still, Spruce thought about them a great deal, hoping to grow up like them.

Despite his thoughts about his future, Spruce was quite happy just being alive and a seedling, growing day by day, a shoot covered with fine hairs and with needle leaves spread and evenly scattered. These needles were four angled with short, fine points. Inside Spruce's deep, blue-green needles, the miracle of photosynthesis, or building with the energy of light and with the soil nutrients from his root system, was going on. In this process, Spruce's living matter was being formed from air, water, and nutrients..

Through countless pores or stomata on the surface of Spruce's needles, air entered the leaves and gave up some of its carbon dioxide. This air chemical united with the chlorophyll in leaf cells. Through a series of reactions, with sunlight supplying the energy, it combined with water and nutrients to form sugar or dextrose. Some of the dextrose then combined with nitrogen to form amino acids, the building blocks from which proteins are made and on which all life, plant and animal, depends. The remaining dextrose was used for conversion into starch, fats, and other substances that were also necessary for Spruce as a source of energy for life processes like respiration. But real growth came from the proteins that the process of photosynthesis created. As in all plant life, Spruce's cells could not grow and divide without proteins. Without the capacity to produce proteins, animals have to depend on plant life for this vital substance of life.

Yet for photosynthesis, growth, and other life processes to occur, an ample amount of water and mineral nutrients are needed. This was supplied by Spruce's root system. Water, containing mineral nutrients, was absorbed by Spruce's roots, pushed into the sapwood, and then pulled up to the needles. The pull was caused by evaporation from pores in the needles and was called transpiration. The energy for this dramatic process, as with photosynthesis, was solar energy, which causes the evaporation. This evaporation created a tremendous pull on the tiny strands of water in the sapwood. The pull, in turn, caused a movement of water in Spruce from roots to shoot tip. Large amounts of water were contained in all of Spruce's tissues. There could not be life or growth without it.

Through photosynthesis and with the help of nitrogen, water, and mineral nutrients, Spruce's body was building. This spot on the mountain meadow provided the right soil, temperature, light, and moisture and Spruce grew rapidly throughout the summer. At the end of the summer, Spruce was a healthy seedling of just over two inches high. But with the first frost in September, life processes began to slow down. Spruce gradually stopped growing as more and more freezing weather came to the mountains with the fall.

Spruce was entering the dormant stage of trees that occurred during the late fall and winter seasons. Photosynthesis, transpiration, and other life processes seemed to end. In many ways, Spruce was inactive or asleep in this dormant or hibernation stage. But the spark and spirit of life were still very present even at this low ebb. As the winter progressed, Spruce was buried under several feet of snow, which was formed lightly around the sleeping seedling and provided a blanket of insulation from the cold mountain winter above.

(2) THE SAPLING

For six winter seasons now, Spruce had been emerging through the winter snows with the beginning of each spring thaw. Now Spruce was over a foot tall, looking very much like a miniature model of a large Engelmann spruce with a pyramid-like shape. Spruce's woody and tapering trunk was not a half inch in diameter at its base, and many small branches grew from its entire length. Numerous needle leaves were borne on peg like projections from Spruce's trunk and branches. The needles would stay for several years before being replaced by new ones. Clusters of bright, new needle growth started to appear at the ends of the branches. With warming weather and sunlight, the needles began actively carrying out photosynthesis. From the dormant stage, Spruce gradually resumed full life processes once more.

Shallow rooted like his other spruce relatives, Spruce also had long, stringy and tough rootlets and a strong tap root for anchoring and for supplying water and mineral nutrients. These rootlets, along with countless roots of other trees and plant life of the mountain forest, served as watershed protectors. As the melting snow gradually released water into drainage on steep slopes, the roots would absorb and the soil would hold much of this water. The roots helped to hold fragile soil in place so that it would not be eroded or washed away. These soils would gradually release much of the stored water to continue on its way, entering the streams below in a stable, continuous flow over the summer.

With melted snow waters seeping into his roots by osmosis, Spruce could feel life begin to flow. Amid patches of snow here and there, the mountain meadow was again starting to emerge and awaken in a chorus of life. Several glacier lilies were already in bloom at the edge of a nearby snow bank. One of the earliest of mountain wildflowers, the lilies, with brilliant yellow and nodding flowers, would soon disappear after a short growing season. Where the snow had receded, new, green grass was appearing. Shrubs like Rocky Mountain juniper and serviceberry had pushed through branches, and new growth pointed toward the inviting spring sunlight. The white of the snow and green of new plant growth gave a fresh and vibrant contrast to the mountain landscape.

What appeared to be a small snow patch was rapidly moving here and there across the meadow. Spruce was puzzled, observing the mysterious ball of snow approach a nearby serviceberry. It was a large bird covered with pure white feathers, a partridge-like grouse of the mountains, a ptarmigan. Spruce noticed that the ptarmigan had stiff, tufted feathers covering his legs and toes for protection from the snow, ice, and cold. Watching the interesting bird peck at the serviceberry, Spruce found himself wanting to talk to this strange bird.

Getting up his courage, Spruce said, "Hope that you are not going to eat me too."

Glancing at Spruce, the ptarmigan replied, "Not unless I was really starved. I tried a tree like you once. Rather disagreeable taste and smell. Nope, I'll stick with plants that are good to eat. I survived all winter here by browsing and digging up shrubs, lichens, willows, and leaves and I surely am not going to try an Engelmann spruce like you, particularly now that it's getting to be spring."

Feeling relief, Spruce asked, "Say, how come you are all white like the snow?"

The ptarmigan replied, "I always turn white like this in the wintertime. If I didn't, then predators like mountain lion or eagles would be able to catch and eat me without any trouble. Haven't you ever heard of protection coloration?" Spruce did not answer so the ptarmigan went on, "Well, it's color that protects you–sort of a natural camouflage. A mountain lion or fox can't tell the difference between me and the snow. I even burrow into it when I sleep. But, with the snow starting to disappear now, my plumage will change to gray. And I'll look just like a rock or boulder up here. It's the way I adapt to seasons up in the mountains–I just change colors to blend with them."

Spruce commented, "That sounds very useful."

"It is," said the ptarmigan, "except when I'm molting or changing my feathers. Then, I'm both gray and white and the predators can spot me more easily. I have to watch it then. I'll soon be starting to molt now that spring is coming again."

Spruce felt concern for the friendly grouse and said, "Gee, I sure hope that they do not catch you. Still, it would be kind of nice to change colors like you do."

Chuckling, the ptarmigan said, "Well, I really don't see how it would help you to survive if you could change the color of your needles. You haven't any predators after you, now, do you?" Spruce answered, "Not really, but a friend of mine, a yarrow, once told me about cutting down trees like me for lumber." Still chuckling, the ptarmigan said, "I don't think you'll have to worry about that for a long time with your size. Well, I've got to be going–see you another time."

As the spring progressed, more and more wildflowers emerged with the receding snow. The meadow became covered with showy petals of brilliantly colored flowers. When the ptarmigan stopped by once in a while to feed and chat, Spruce noticed that he was molting and had a unique combination of gray and white feathers.

Spruce wondered how it would be to fly like the ptarmigan and other birds. High overhead, Spruce would notice a golden eagle wheel about in its persistent search for prey. Several little rosy finches were fluttering and darting around here and there, feeding on the still insects that had been numbed with the mountain cold and blown up from the valleys.

Spruce greatly admired the flight of a Clark's nutcracker that occasionally visited the meadow. The large, gray-bodied bird would display its black wings and tail and large white patches as it flew in long graceful dips. One time, the handsome bird alighted on a serviceberry near Spruce and began pecking on some of the buds with his large and powerful looking beak. Spruce called out, "Hi, there! I've been watching you fly. You certainly are beautiful and graceful flying around here the way you do." Feeling flattered, the bird replied, "Thanks, little tree. My name is Bill, the neighborhood Clark's nutcracker. What's your name?"

Spruce replied, "Spruce. By the way, why are birds like you called Clark's nutcrackers?"

After pecking at some buds, Bill replied, "A long time ago, a man by the name of William Clark was an early explorer to the Northwest with the Lewis-Clark expedition. He and another man by the name of Lewis, led the party. William Clark must have seen some of my ancestors cracking pine cones or nuts with their large and strong beaks. So he added nutcracker to his name and gave it to us. Hence, the name Clark's nutcracker. I kind of like it."

Bill paused as he spotted a small but juicy insect on one of the serviceberry leaves. With a quick jump, Bill had the insect and gulped him down. A bit taken aback, Spruce commented, "Poor little fellow! He never had a chance." With a satisfied look, Bill said, "Mmmm, he was pretty good too, but I guess he has just joined the food chain."

Puzzled, Spruce asked, "Food chain—what's that?" Bill answered, "It's a chain of eating and being eaten relationships. We're all in it in one form or another. Take that bug that I just ate—and he was rather good tasting—he was eating the leaves of the serviceberry right?"

Spruce answered, "Yes, I guess so," while wondering how the

serviceberry felt with having its leaves eaten by the insect and then Bill.

Hopping closer to Spruce, Bill continued, "O.K., plant life like you and the serviceberry are primary producers of matter and capture energy through photosynthesis. No animal can do this so we have to get it from you plants. Hey, don't worry, I'm not going to eat you. Trees like you just don't taste good."

Spruce commented, "That's what the ptarmigan said, too. But go on."

"Well," said Bill, "animals like me get our food and energy from eating plants and eating each other. The bug, or plant eater, I just ate had eaten the food and energy of the service berry–so now this stuff was in the bug. Got it?"

Spruce replied, "Yes, but you also eat plant leaves for food."

Pausing patiently and tilting his head, Bill said, "Let's not get too complicated. A lot of animals are what they call omnivorous which means they can eat both plant and animal life. But let's get back to the bug. I ate it and it contains the plant matter and energy. Now, if, heaven forbid, something like a coyote should eat me, then the service-berry's food and energy would be passed along to it. But the bug, myself, and the coyote would burn off most of the leaves' food and energy in living. We would only store a small amount of it so the food chain is really shaped like a pyramid– with a lot on the bottom and a small amount passed on to the top for the large flesh eaters or carnivores, like coyotes and mountain lions. In short, the energy flow of the food chain gets more and more reduced the higher up you go."

Trying to picture all this, Spruce asked, "But what about the coyote?"

"Well," answered Bill, "it would eventually die, I guess. Then bacteria and fungi would break it down to raw material to become part of the soil. Then plants will absorb soil nutrients and off we go again into the food chain.

"That sounds fascinating," Spruce marveled. "I never knew that there was such a thing as a food chain."

Bill said, "But you are in it, too. Birds and other animals will be eating the cones and seeds that you eventually produce. And some may even try to eat parts of you. Don't forget, with your photosynthesis, you are a primary producer of the stuff they need."

Spruce became a bit anxious upon hearing this and said, "I didn't know the food chain would come that close to home." Laughing, Bill commented, 'Well, what about your roots? They are getting nutrients from soil composed of living and dead things of the food chain. And when you finally die someday—we all do—then bacteria, microorganisms, and fungi will break down your wood fibers along with insects and worms; they will all turn you into organic materials of soil for other plants to grow in."

Spruce lapsed into a serious and sad mood. Realizing this, Bill said, "Spruce, cheer up and enjoy it. You are just a part of the old food chain that we are all in. That's how energy from the sun flows through the living things of our planet earth. Every living thing is in this web of life and energy flow, even after it dies." Reflecting, Spruce said, "What about that rock over there? Is it in our food chain?" In a series of several large hops, Bill landed on the rock and looked at the green and orange lichen covering the rock. Nodding his large beak and head, he said, "Yep, I guess it is. This rock will eventually turn to soil because of the lichen on it as well as weathering.

Puzzled, Spruce commented, "That's hard to believe. What are lichens, anyway?"

Pecking and eating some of the lichen, Bill paused and replied, "They are sometimes called pioneer plants. They can grow right on the smooth surface of a rock like this one without any soil."

Spruce exclaimed, "That's amazing! I thought all plants had to have soil for their roots like I do. And they don't even look like a plant—more like some kind of green and orange covering over the rock. It's hard to believe that they are a plant."

Bill said, "But they are. In fact, lichens are made up of two different types of plants living together in a working partnership:

algae and fungi. A blue-green algae lives among the tangled threads of fungi to form a lichen. The algae, through its green chlorophyll, makes food for both of them through photosynthesis. The fungi–something like a mushroom–does not contain chlorophyll. But its spongy material holds both to the rock and supplies the algae part with water and nutrients–just like a root would. Both plants benefit from one another and this working together is called symbiosis. And so they can survive on the bare rock as lichens. Really unusual plants, but not that good to eat–passable though, I guess."

Spruce watched as Bill flew and landed back at the serviceberry, then called, "But you still haven't told me how rock becomes soil because of the lichens."

Pausing after pecking at a lead bud, Bill said, "That's right, and you got me off the track with your plant questions. Anyway, the lichen secretes acids that work on the rock and dissolve some of the minerals in it that are used by the algae part of it. The rock becomes the lichen's soil and nutrients something like what you need and use in your soil.. With enough of this carbolic acid dissolving away, the rock starts to crumble."

Spruce commented, "Seems like that would take a long time. I haven't noticed much of a change in that rock since I've been here."

Agreeing with a nod of his head, Bill continued, "It does take a very, very long time. And weathering helps a lot too with rain, snow, wind, thawing and freezing, and heat expansion, working on the rock along with the lichen acid. Invading mosses and other small plants will eventually start growing on the broken and cracked places of the rock and use dead lichen for soil."

Hopping to a spot next to Spruce, Bill continued, "And then larger plants and trees like you will grow on the dead mosses and small plants. This is called plant succession: one type of plant replacing another. Their root pressures will cause more cracking and splitting of the rock. Gradually, soil is formed from the crumbling rock and from the dead and living plant and animal materials. It takes about 500 years to form one inch of topsoil this way."

Spruce reflected, "Gosh, that sounds like a long time!!"

Bill said, "It is, but some Engelmann spruce like you get to be that old and older. Maybe you will too–if you're lucky. If you do, you will have seen another inch of topsoil from here. You are already contributing to it with some of the needles that you are shedding."

Spruce observed the few needles that had fallen. The needles had stayed on for several years before dying and dropping to be replaced by new needles. With Bill's teaching about the food chain, soil formation and other things, Spruce felt even more related to the living world.

Getting ready to fly, Bill called, "Hey, I better get going or my mate will be mad at me for not helping with the kids. Those four want all the insects and seeds we can bring them–and then some. It's hard work to loosen and grab off a spruce or pine cone with my feet and then knock the scales off with my beak. But they really gobble up the seeds when I haul them to the nest. Guess I needed a break. Enjoyed visiting with you. I'll drop by again sometime, Spruce."

Saying goodbye, Spruce watched Bill gradually disappear in a graceful flight across the meadow and through the trees of the forest.

(3) THE POLE

With the passing of fifty seasons, Spruce was now in the pole stage and even had visits with Bill's offspring over the years. Growing rapidly as a healthy young tree under good conditions with plenty of sunlight, Spruce was now forty feet high and over a half foot in diameter at breast height. Spruce's trunk had a pole-like appearance inside the lush growth of branches and countless needles. In human growth rate and life span, Spruce was now approaching his teen years. His blue-green conical shape added handsome beauty and noble character to the quiet meadow.

For some time now, some of Spruce's energy and food materials had been going into seed production. Near the top of this conifer, cone buds would appear in July before flowering the following spring. All Engelmann spruce produce both male and female flowers separately. Each is tiny and circular. The male flowers are dark purple and the female flowers are bright scarlet. In June, the male flowers dry out and fall soon after their pollen is shed and spread by the wind. The female flowers receive the pollen and become fertilized. By August the female flowers develop into cylindrical, light brown cones about two inches long. In the fall, small, dark-brown winged seeds are shed from the cone and spread by the wind. By early winter, the cones had dropped from Spruce; large crops of cones and seeds were produced, not every year, but in intervals of three or four years.

Birds and other wildlife would eat many of Spruce's cones and seeds. One August of a good seed year, Spruce got to know Red, a Chickaree squirrel, quite well. Red would occasionally climb to the top of Spruce to reach the highest cones. He would clip a twig holding the cones, watch it fall, and then proceed to the ground to eat the seeds in the cones or to bury them in storage holes. Spruce would usually protest this treatment, but to no avail. Red would chatter and scold that Spruce had plenty of cones and that it was not really hurting that much. Red would also point out that he was providing Spruce with good company and conversation for the food that Spruce was providing.

Spruce could not help liking the friendly, chattering Chickaree or red squirrel, despite his cone raids. A bit mischievous, Red was entertaining and full of character. His small body and twitching tail vibrated with energy and life. He was very agile in leaping and scampering here and there. Red loved to scold in a very impudent manner.

One time, when a fox came into the meadow, Red became very excited. From a safe perch in Spruce, he started a scolding chatter that grew increasingly louder. Realizing that any prey in the vicinity was thoroughly warned, the fox departed in disgust. Red then continued with boastful chatter.

One fine fall day, Red hopped across the meadow and swiftly shot up Spruce's trunk to the higher branches. Spruce remarked, "Oh no, don't tell me you are after more of my cones again."

Red replied, "Why not. It's my niche to do this type of thing."

Curious, Spruce asked, "Before, Red, you always used excuses like plenty of cones, good company, and not hurting me much. What is this niche business?"

Starting to clip a small branch with cones on it, Red replied, "I got it from another Chickaree squirrel I was talking to the other day. He said that a niche is what a living thing does in a community of other living things or ecosystem. It's the role it plays. And right now, I'm playing the role of consuming some of your energy in the food chain. How's that?"

"Sounds interesting," Spruce thought aloud. "What you're trying to say is that we all have a place in this mountain forest and meadow based on how we live and get food from it."

Chattering softly, Red said, "Right. And niche says what our relationships are with the community and with one another. You and I are both different kinds of living things and we both have different roles to play like other living things around here. If we were all the same, we would all be trying to get the same food and competing for it. Nothing would survive and we would not have a living community like we do. That's why we all have different niches in our relationships. Just think if we were all squirrels like me or trees like you."

Spruce contemplated this point while watching Red continue to gnaw at one small branch with cones on it. Finally, the branch fell to the ground, and Red rapidly descended to land near the fallen branch. Captivated by the delicious looking cones, Red forgot to look and smell about before plunging into his dinner. Without warning, an animal about the size of a bear cub pounced on Red like a shot. Before Red could even utter a cry or fight back, the powerful jaws of a wolverine had instantly crushed the life from his small body. In nothing flat, Red's body was rapidly gulped down by the wolverine.

Shocked at the scene, Spruce felt a deep sense of sadness at the fate of his small friend. Yet, he was fascinated by the new and strange looking creature; he had never seen anything quite like it before. The wolverine looked like a squat, broad, but small bear with a bushy tail and short, bowed legs. Its long and coarse-haired coat was blackish-brown with a chestnut stripe on each side for a skunk-like appearance.

Spruce learned later that an Indian name for the wolverine was "skunk-bear." The wolverine was not a bear at all but the largest member of the weasel family; it was also the strongest as well as the most resourceful and cunning of this family of predators.

Deciding to relax a bit after her meal, the wolverine lay down next to Spruce. With a loping gait in her persistent search for prey, Gula, the wolverine, had covered almost thirty miles by this late afternoon. Too slow and awkward to overtake fast creatures she had been watching and waiting for Red to be off guard so she could take him by surprise. This was how she usually took her prey of rodents, birds, young deer, and about anything that she could get her powerful teeth and claws into, including carrion. Gula had poor eyesight like all wolverines. But her powerful muscles, keen sense of smell, and tireless abilities usually were successful in getting enough prey for her enormous appetite.

Taking in the warm sunlight of the meadow by Spruce, Gula reflected that this was much better than the cold winter and snow. Never hibernating, Gula had continued her relentless hunting during the winter over the deep mountain snows. The thick and coarse hairs on her feet had acted as snowshoes as she methodically plodded and roamed the snow-covered, high country. She would usually do quite well even in the hard winters in her determined and relentless search for food.

Gula could still remember a day last winter when she had come upon a large mountain lion eating a freshly killed deer. Without hesitation, she attacked and drove off the mountain lion which was several times larger than herself. Eating all she could of the deer carcass, she had then used his musk glands to apply an offensive odor to the rest of it so no other animal would get it.

A solitary, rare and courageous animal, Gula had always traveled alone since she was a year old when driven away by her mother. She asked no quarter and gave none as she faced winters, mountain lions, bears, or anything else that she encountered.

Debating whether or not to talk to this strange creature, Spruce finally called out, "Why did you kill that poor Chickaree squirrel? He was my friend."

Gula replied, "Sorry about that. I guess I was just hungry like

I usually am. I really had nothing against him. It's just my nature to take prey like the squirrel."

Spruce commented, "But it seems sad to me for him to be killed."

Gula retorted , "Well, I'm sure that he killed his share of birds. They do love to eat them, you know."

Spruce reflected, "I suppose so. Guess I'll never understand why some of you animals are always killing and eating each other. I've seen it happen many times over the years and it does seem cruel to me."

Scratching her ear with a hind leg, Gula finally said, "Well, I don't think it is being cruel in taking our prey. How else are we going to get our food? Animals like me that eat other animals are predators and it's just part of the natural processes. It's our niche."

Surprised, Spruce said, "That's strange. Red was just telling me about niches before you ate him."

Gula continued,"Well, it's true. Predators have their niches and relationships in the living community like everything else. We are flesh eaters, or carnivores, who usually eat other animals that get their food from plants. That puts us predators at the top of the food chain, and there are a lot fewer of us than other living things. It is something like a pyramid—the higher up you go, the smaller it gets with less food and energy being passed along. There has to be a lot of plants and plant eating animals to support the smaller numbers of predators like us. But keep in mind that all we are doing is eating other animals to stay alive."

Spruce reflected, "Well, I guess I can understand that. But I still feel bad about poor old Red."

Shaking her head, Gula said, "Well, you'll get over it. And there are plenty of Chickaree squirrels around to make friends with. In fact, one of the things that we predators do is to keep down rodent populations such as squirrels so they don't get out of hand. Otherwise, they would eat up everything in sight during a high population cycle. Just think! If there were thousands of Reds running here—they would eat this place out of house and home. We also take a lot of sick and weak, or older prey, which improves the breeding stock of wildlife. But the big point is that we take what is available and what we can catch. And Red was just unwary enough to be available when I could catch him. In doing this, we usually keep things healthy, including prey animals. I guess you could say that we are a part of the balance of nature."

Thinking about this, Spruce noticed that Gula was getting restless and asked, "What's up?'

Loping off in her wild and free manner, Gula called back, "Just smelled a nice snowshoe rabbit, and I'm hungry as ever so off I go. See you." Gula quickly bounded from sight into the forest.

Spruce wondered if Gula would get the rabbit, when suddenly a sharp cry and scramble was followed by silence. Spruce knew that this rare, strange, and fascinating predator had struck again. But now, Spruce would be able to understand her more.

Through conversations with animals like Gula, Red, Bill, and others, Spruce was constantly learning and understanding more and more about that which surrounded him in the mountain forest and meadow. All of them, including himself, were very much a part of the web of life with its niches and relationships.

For Red and Gula, it had been the photosynthesis of Spruce's needles that produced the food and energy of the cones that Red had eaten. Some of this same food and energy used by Red was now in Gula as another link of the food chain. When Gula died, it would be passed on to birds and animals that fed on her and on to the organic material of the soil. Others plants and trees would then use it in photosynthesis for food and energy which, in turn, would be used by other animals. It seemed to Spruce that the food chain could go on forever.

Spruce was constantly impressed with the diversity of life forms and how each adapted to the habitat and seasons of the mountain forest. In observing other trees, Spruce noticed that certain types would usually grow at certain elevations. In the lower elevation, or Montane zone, the climate was warmer and dryer. Here, Ponderosa pine, with its long dull green needles, Lodgepole pine, with its tall, straight trunk and with most of its foliage at the top, and quaking aspen, with its white bark and trembling small leaves, were dominant and abundant. These and other forms of life of the Montane zone could adapt best to the lower elevation conditions beneath him.

In the middle zone, or Taiga, where Spruce lived, conditions were much colder, with freezing temperatures for almost half the year with the increase in elevation up the mountain. Yet thick, abundant stands of Engelmann spruce and silvery-barked subalpine fir occurred in broad belts of continuous forest. They, like the dominant trees of the Montane zone, were the climax vegetation that had reached a steady and stable state and could survive indefinitely under these conditions. Climax trees were mainly dependent on the climate for maintaining themselves. Like Spruce, they were adapted to the conditions and were in tune with climate so they thrived in their particular zone.

Above the Taiga zone, Spruce observed the alpine meadows, or tundra, which was the highest zone with vegetation before the rocks and snow of the mountaintops. At these high elevations, with extreme cold and strong winds, the ground was permanently frozen-with the exception of a thin layer that thawed during the summer for about three months. No trees could adapt or survive in this arctic world.

But on the lower boundaries of the tundra, Spruce witnessed the struggle for life at the timberline. There, eccentric whitebark pine, with its flexible, segmented branches, and long, swishing needles, illustrated nature's survival qualities. To resist the severe winds, the supple trunk of the whitebark pines lay horizontally on the ground and sprawled over rocks like a serpent. Very slow-growing, many of the small whitebark pine were several hundred years old.

Spruce was completely fascinated by the beauty of the flowers of the actual tundra beyond this strange timberline. Amid the dwarfed grasses, hedges, shrubs, herbs, and mosses, a virtual sea of colorful and beautiful tundra wildflowers covered the alpine meadows. The vast carpets of showy flowers were myriads of low, cushion-like flower clumps that hugged the ground to avoid the intense wind and to conserve moisture. The variety of flowers and colors dazzled Spruce as he observed golden alpine avens, dark purple alpine forget-me-nots, pale yellow alpine anemones, brilliant red King's Crowns, lavender fairy primroses, pink moss campions, blue skypilots, white alpine phloxes, bright yellow alpine wallflowers, and many others.

The plant clumps of the flowers were very slow growing and ranged in ages from a hundred to several hundred years old. Like the dominant trees in others zones, they had adapted themselves to become the climax vegetation of their harsh environment. Many had amazing adaptations to protect themselves from loss of vital fluids in the cold, dry air and strong winds. Some plants had coverings of soft, hairy "fur" or waxy material while others would store liquids in their thick, fleshy parts. Still others would have a hard or leathery outer coat. Their reduced size and ground hugging postures helped to conserve their energies as well as to protect themselves from the winds.

By managing to adapt to this high, cold region, the tundra plants protected the fragile mountain soil from erosion. They contributed to the watershed by storing water, preventing rapid runoff, and releasing the water slowly throughout the summer like a sponge. Spruce saw many forms of wildlife, including bighorn sheep and mountain goats, graze on these unique, delicate and fragile plants over the summer.

Spruce surveyed the different zones of his living world and noticed that the boundaries between them were indistinct and irregular. It was often difficult to tell exactly where one began and another left off. These hazy boundaries were the "battlegrounds" or ecotones, between the different trees and plants of different zones. Often, invading trees and plants from one zone found favorable conditions in this boundary area and made inroads into the edges of another zone by replacing those already there. But this succession or constant change of the different zones would eventually produce a stable association that was in balance and order with the conditions present. Spruce, without fail, could make out the definitive patterns of the life zones despite their complicated transitional ecotones.

(4) THE TREE

With the passing of another fifty seasons, the different trees and plants of the life zones had remained pretty much the same. But new trees had appeared and the older trees like Spruce were getting a lot larger. Still steadily growing, Spruce was now 70 feet high and over 14 inches in diameter at breast height. Spruce's trunk, or bole, no longer had a pole-like appearance but was thick and solid appearing. It had a buttressed base and gradually tapered along its entire length.

In human growth rate and life span, Spruce was now in the late teen years as a young adult tree. His large and impressive appearance as a healthy blue-green giant was accented in color and form by this prominent place in the meadow and mountain landscape. With Spruce's meadow near the edge of the mountain cliff overlook, his noble features and beauty could be seen from afar.

Without having to compete for sunlight in the open meadow, Spruce had grown faster and larger than the other spruce in the nearby forest. Throughout most of their lives, the other Engelmann spruce had to compete for the limited sunlight that filtered through the semi-closed canopies of branches and needles of the older and larger trees, including mixtures of Subalpine fir. Because the Engelmann spruce were very tolerant of shade and poor sunlight, the forest contained spruce of all ages and sizes, varying from seedlings, saplings, and poles to larger trees. Yet, small, suppressed trees would show a remarkable ability to respond with rapid growth when they finally did get plenty of sunlight.

Without the full sunlight that Spruce was getting, the other trees of the same age concentrated their energy and growth toward the available sunlight. As a result, their trunks or boles were somewhat thinner though sometimes taller than Spruce's trunk. As they grew, sunlight would not reach their lower limbs and needles, causing them to die off through natural pruning. In the forest, the lower parts of the larger trees had many dead limbs on them. In the meadow, most of Spruce's lower limbs were alive and vigorous from abundant sunlight and formed the broad base of a pyramid-like form.

From this open vantage point in the meadow, Spruce sometimes wondered what it would be like to live in the nearby forest. Typical of the Engelmann spruce-subalpine fir association of the Taiga zone, the inside of the surrounding forest appeared like a mysterious twilight in places with the shade from its dense canopy. In other places, shafts of sunlight were gleaming through openings in the upper branches to lighten and brighten the ground as in a vast cathedral. Spruce could easily spot the subalpine fir with their silvery bark, flattened needles, and erect dark-colored cones as they blended in form with the more dominant and more abundant Engelmann spruce. The forest had a certain captivating aura and natural strength about it.

Like Spruce, the forest trees grew straight from the ground to their tip without forking. The branches were thrust out at right angles in regularly shaped whorls that gave the trees the forms of sharp spires. Many of the branches interlocked with branches of other, nearby trees. The different ages and sizes of the trees were almost amusing to Spruce; he realized how the younger ones would mimic the larger ones, becoming miniature models of them.

With twice as much rainfall and snow in the Taiga zone as

compared to other zones, the abundant moisture supported the luxuriant tree life of the forest. Yet sunlight was a limiting factor on survival and growth, and all of the trees of the forest appeared to be quietly struggling to get enough of it. Spruce was glad not to have a worry about sunlight and was again thankful for his lucky spot in the meadow.

In Spruce's meadow, there were plenty of shrubs, herbs, and wildflowers. But on the forest floor this type of plant life was limited. The shade from the dense canopy of interlocking branches did not permit very much sunlight to reach low growing plants. And many of the plants had difficulty in starting in the thick carpet of needles, which disintegrated very slowly.

Yet where some sunlight was concentrated, shrubs like juniper with its grayish-purple berries, mountain maple, mountain ash with clusters of white flowers, kinnikinnick or bearberry with its bright red berries, orange-red buffalo berries, and honeysuckle with pairs of yellow flowers were present. The lighted areas also had wild flowers like the white globe flower with its cup-shaped flower of a cream color, monkshood with its blue, helmeted flower, and Parry primrose with its clusters of bright purple flowers.

But some unique flowers could thrive in the shadowed depths of the forest where the light was very dim. In the far and dark recesses of the forest, Spruce observed fairy slippers, a dainty orchid with rose-colored flowers in the shape of a tiny slipper; pink pyrola, a herb with five thick white petals on its flowers; spotted coral root, a saprophyte plant that lives off decaying vegetation through a fungus and bears purple spotted orchid flowers, and twinflower, a dense mat that sent forth forked stems bearing a pair of pink, bell-shaped flowers. In the depths of the forest, these and other flowers added to the beauty and fascination of the nature wonderland.

Over the seasons, Spruce noticed that most of the wildlife used the forest for cover or stalking. Grazing animals like the mule deer and elk would find only limited ground cover for their food in the forest. They would use the natural opening of the forest or open meadows where there was plenty of browse. But they and other wildlife needed the shadowy, protecting forest for cover so they could hide from predators and the weather.

Predator animals, like the mountain lion and marten, needed the shaded, thick forest to conceal themselves while stalking or wailing for their prey. One time, Spruce had watched a mountain lion crouched and hidden in the trees near a game trail in the forest. As an unwary mule deer approached, the mountain lion thrust itself forward to attack and kill the surprised deer.

Many animals and birds were frequently seen in the forest by Spruce, particularly those that fed on tree seeds and buds. Chicka-ree squirrels and other rodents were frequently nearby. Birds like Clark's nutcrackers, grouse, jays, woodpeckers, and others were usually in the vicinity. Over the seasons, Spruce had observed count-less deer, elk, and moose traveling through the forest. Occasion-ally, predators like mountain lions, wolves, black bears, and mar-tens passed through the forest. The forest was a living thorough-fare for the wildlife that needed and used it in many ways.

Spruce recalled seeing only two other wolverines besides Gula over the many seasons. Perhaps wolverines were not only rare, but extremely rare wildlife. Yet, there had been at least ten different grizzly bears in the area. While reflecting on this, Spruce was very surprised when a grizzly bear suddenly appeared.

Startled, he watched the grizzly meander slowly through the forest in a lumbering gait, making its way into the meadow. Spruce could easily tell that it was a grizzly by its saucer face, silver-tipped brown coat, humped back, and long claws. But this bear was the largest Spruce had ever seen. The massive animal was over seven feet long and weighed about several hundred pounds.

In his perpetual search for food, Ursus had traveled more than twelve miles that day. He had fed mainly on plants, berries, and roots. But Ursus did manage to dig out and catch a marmot and a ground squirrel earlier in the day while ranging lower in the Mon-tane zone. As he moved through the meadow, his huge head, with a broad, dished face, swung from side to side to sniff the wind.

Like all grizzly bears, his eyesight was very poor. He relied mainly on his sensitive and keen nose when he examined the countryside.

With humped shoulders and short back legs, Ursus seemed to be constantly trudging uphill. As the largest carnivore of the northern Rockies, his diet still consisted mainly of vegetation material with meat, including carrion, when readily available. He was powerfully built, heavily muscled, and had large teeth and claws. He appeared fearless and majestic. In hunting and feeding, Ursus was an opportunist and would eat almost anything.

Although nearly always hungry, Ursus was carefree and happy as he followed his nose and constantly searched out things to eat. He grazed on some of the meadow grass, and clawed at an underground den of field mice until he finally caught two through the large hole that he dug. Ursus got most of his food by using his claws as a pick and shovel. Finding some berries on a nearby shrub, Ursus proceeded to strip them from the branches with the long, sharp claws of his forefeet and to cram them into his mouth rapidly. Unable to find any more berries, Ursus licked his lips in relish over the small dessert and then ambled over toward Spruce.

When he arrived, Ursus stood on his hind legs and reached through Spruce with his fore paws. He then made a long slashes on Spruce's trunk with his long, slightly curved, but very sharp claws after he had reached as high as he could. When Ursus dropped back down on his fours, he surveyed the long slashes with pride and satisfaction.

Shocked and indignant, Spruce shouted, "Why did you do that for? Are you trying to destroy me?"

Ursus calmly paused for a moment and then replied, "Don't get excited. I was just putting up a sign to mark my territory. A lot of animals use some kind of markings or scent to advertise that an area belongs only to them. Even birds do this by their singing. It's the way that we can establish and defend an area from other animals as our territory, particularly animals that might compete with us. Otherwise, there would not be enough space for feeding and mating or just being alone."

Spruce said, "Well, I sure hope that you don't claw me up much more. Just under my bark is the only real living tissue that I have, you know. And it has to transport water and food. If you clawed all the way around my trunk, I would be girdled or cut off between my needles and roots. And that would be the end–just like that dead tree over there. A porcupine gnawed all the way around its trunk and killed it."

Swaying his head from side to side, Ursus said, "You don't have to worry about me. I may put a claw mark or two on you some other time, but you are a good sized tree. I happen to be pretty good sized too. Other smaller bears will see my claw marks way up there and leave the country right away. You see, I need a large area for all my needs, and I am not about to let other bears get into it. That's why I mark big trees like you once in a while. Just putting up no trespassing signs, I guess."

Sighing with relief, Spruce said, "Could you not climb up and put higher marks? Then other bears would really think that you were a lot bigger than you are."

Chuckling, Ursus replied, "No way. I used to be able to climb when I was a cub with my mother. My claws are too long and straight-like now to use in climbing. My smaller cousins, the black bears, can usually climb no matter how old they are. Their claws are much more curbed and shorter. Regardless, other bears will spot my territory signs of grizzly claw marks in trees. They will be able to tell a lot about me, including how big I am, by the marks. Some may even try to see if they can reach as high as I did just to see if they have a chance to take over my territory with a fight. But, almost always, they'll take off soon enough. They usually get the message of no trespassing pretty quick."

Spruce commented, "Well, being as big as you are, you must not have to worry much about other bears and animals."

Reflecting for a moment, Ursus said, "Not really–except when it comes to human beings. You know, those odd animals that always walk around on their hind legs. Surely you must have seen some, haven't you?" Spruce replied, "Yes, I think I know what you mean. I remember seeing several of them over the years, but they never came very close. They were strange looking–certainly not like other animals that I've seen around here. When I was very young, I saw some with red faces, but the ones that I saw after that all had white faces. They sure are strange looking creatures."

Ursus shook his body and said, "And also the most dangerous. Did you happen to notice that some of them carried long sticks? With those things, they can cause a loud noise, like thunder, that can hurt or kill anything that they point it at. When I was a cub, they did that to my mother and sister. Both of them just fell dead as I ran away. Whenever I can smell or hear human beings, I get away as fast as I can. I also learned to stay away from anything that has their odd smell on it. One time, I ate some carrion with a human smell in it and a pair of jaws clanged together on my fur. But I tore it loose. I fear very little, but I'm very afraid of those human beings."

Spruce said, "But, with your large size, teeth, and claws, it seems to me that you could really let them have it. As I recall, they did not appear very large or powerful."

Ursus scratched aimlessly at the ground for a moment, and then said, "That may be, but as long as I can get away without fighting them, I will. There is something terrifying and unnatural about them and their dangerous sticks. And I want to avoid them if at all possible. All I hope is that I get some kind of warning in smell or sound that they are coming so they don't surprise or provoke me into an attack. And even then, I think I would try to retire from the scene as long as I could keep my dignity."

Looking up at Spruce, Ursus continued, "And what about you? When the human beings come up to cut you down for lumber, you won't be able to run away."

Spruce did not reply right away. But suddenly remembering other warnings like this, he said "But the human beings have not even come close to me in all my life". "O.K., it's true that I can't run away like you can, but I don't think they will ever come way out here and try to cut me down."

Ursus sadly shook his head and said, 'Don't worry, Spruce, the human beings will be here–in this very spot–sooner or later. They get everywhere, and they do what they want."

Worried, Spruce asked, "But why can't they leave us alone?"

Ursus replied, "I don't know. I guess it's something about the human animal that drives them to kill or ruin everything that's wild and free. They must have some kind of need to conquer and take over all the land and living things for themselves. In my case, they have driven me out of three territories that I've established so far. And this one is about the last that I know about. If they drive me out of this area, I just don't know what I'm going to do."

Curious, Spruce asked, "But could you not live around them by avoiding them. What do they do that drives you away?"

Ursus cringed for a moment and replied, "You mean what don't they do! When they come into an area, most of the big trees like you are cut down with loud, noisy things. The noise terrifies wild creatures for miles. Then they start building big trails with huge, and still noisier things. They load the trees on other big things that go back and forth on the big trails."

With a sad sigh, Ursus continued, "But that's only the beginning. With the logging, there were not too many human beings. But with the big trails, they really start pouring into the area on all sorts of strange things that make a lot of noise. It becomes impossible to avoid them or their scent. Then there are those strange, big caves that they put up here and there with horrible thorns strung together. And most of them have their long sticks that shoot lightning and thunder. The only thing I could do was to move out. Besides, I can't stand to be near or around them anyway. Would you like all that around here?"

Spruce shuddered at the thought of logging and what human beings would do to the meadow and forest. Then Spruce exclaimed, "No! It sounds terrible. Isn't there any way of stopping those humans?"

With a wry smile, Ursus said, "Well, I suppose that I could attack them and run off a few. But that would not do any good.

They'd only hunt me down and kill me with a lot more humans.
No, if an area is to remain wild and free, it will be because the
humans want it that way. Given problems and time, they can get
anywhere and destroy it. So it's only the humans that can decide
not to disturb and ruin something, including this place and us."

While Ursus grazed on some nearby grass and hedges, Spruce
thought about experiences of all the years and how much there
was to know about the living community and web of life. Spruce
then called Ursus, "Suppose some of those humans start understanding that they are just members of a living community like all
of us. You know, Ursus, that we are all interrelated and interde-
pendent in a web of life. Well, if some of those human beings
understood this, maybe they would have respect and concern for
other living members of the community. Then, maybe they would
not try to destroy and conquer everything—or at least leave some
places alone where everyone can be fellow members of the living
community, including the humans."

Ursus stopped grazing and sat down on his hind quarters. After a pause, he said, "That sounds pretty good, Spruce. But let's
face it. They have conquered and ruined about every place that I
have been during my lifetime. It's hard to see how they are going
to stop with this place. The humans are supposed to be the smart-
est animals, and yet they simply want to take over the land and its
life to suit themselves—regardless of the consequences—even for
themselves. I don't believe that they realize that they are members
of the living community. I guess the humans think that they are
apart from nature. And . . ."

Spruce interrupted, "But they can change, can't they? You
said that they were awfully smart, didn't you?"

Shaking his head angrily, Ursus replied, "Maybe too smart for
their own good! They are plenty smart enough to do what they
darn well please with all their strange noisy and destructive things.
Are they being intelligent, fellow members of the community when
they go around destroying wildlife like me and cutting trees like
you—by ruining our homes and habitats? All they want are the

privileges and demands of using the land in any way that they want to—and when they want to—without any obligations. Are they showing any respect for our lives when they do this?"

Spruce sadly answered, "No, I guess not, Ursus. But still, the humans could reserve some natural and wild places for wildlife like you and trees like me if they wanted to. After all, they don't have to develop everything. And you and other living things do have a right to live just as they do."

Calming down, Ursus said, "Well, let's face it. If they don't reserve some wild places, animals like me will simply become extinct. We'll be gone from the face of the earth for good and nature will not replace us. You see, there are a lot of wildlife like me that simply cannot survive without undisturbed habitat. Some animals, like deer and racoons, can survive quite well living right around the humans and their things—just so they have limited plant cover around for protection and food. But for others, like myself, particularly predators—we simply cannot tolerate much contact with humans and the changes they bring. Right now, there are very few grizzly bears, wolverines, and wolves left. Rare wildlife like us are endangered with very good chances of becoming extinct in the near future if something is not done by the humans. We are in trouble."

"Certainly the humans, intelligent as they are supposed to be, must realize this, don't you think?", Spruce offered.

Ursus replied, "I'm sure some do, but it does not seem to stop them. In your life so far, Spruce, dozens of different kinds of wildlife have become extinct like the prairie wolf, eastern elk, and over a hundred are endangered with becoming extinct like the wolverine and myself. At one time, there was even a plains grizzly bear that lived in the flat lands. As the human beings settled in, they took over their plains habitat and killed almost all of them off. Those that were left fled to remote and isolated mountain and forest areas for protection. I understand my grandfather was a plains grizzly bear. At least, he had a place to flee to then."

Spruce exclaimed, "That sounds tragic! What right do humans have to do that to other animals, not to mention the plants and trees involved? After all, every type of animal is a unique marvel of creation with millions of years of evolution behind its development. It has its own special place and niche in nature's scheme. I can't see what right the humans have to permanently destroy endangered wildlife like you, Ursus. Certainly, they must feel some responsibilities. After all . . ."

Ursus interrupted, "What responsibilities except for themselves and what they think they own? Whenever humans and endangered wildlife come into contact and conflict, the endangered wildlife, like wolves, wolverines, and myself, are considered predators to be destroyed. Even though humans are predators themselves, they can't stand others being predators, too."

Ursus stopped and clawed the ground in disgust. Spruce finally asked, "Why should they object to animals that get their food by eating other animals just as they do?"

Stopping his clawing and sitting down again, Ursus replied, "Well, once in a while, a wolf or grizzly bear like me will take one of those strange, feeble-looking, dumb animals that the humans put out to graze. After all, they are easy to catch. Then the humans will do everything to kill all predators in the vicinity with dogs, traps, poison, and guns. They'll usually do this anyway—even if the predators were just around and not bothering their strange animals. I guess they are also afraid of us and figure that they must wipe out everything that might be a threat in some way. They don't mind killing any predator with teeth."

Spruce considered this and said, "But you would—under some circumstances—would you not attack humans, Ursus? You did say something like this before."

Thinking for awhile, Ursus replied, "Like I said, it would have to be very unusual circumstances. I did charge a couple of humans once when they surprised me without any warnings. But then I turned and ran away—guess my fear of them is much stronger than my pride. And that's why I finally left that territory. But some grizzly bears will remain in their territory even though a lot of humans with their noisy things and feeble animals will take it over. Then it becomes impossible to avoid having bear and human conflicts. And that usually means the end of the grizzly bear. We and the other endangered wildlife have to be left alone in wild places where few humans come—where humans are just visitors to these areas."

"Also, places where they don't cut down trees like me," Spruce agreed. "I have a right to live too, even if I'm not as endangered as you are. Hey, what are you looking at?"

Ursus answered, "At those nice cones of yours. Been watching them for some time, and I would sure like to eat some of the tasty seeds in those cones."

Spruce said, "Well, you said that you can't climb so I don't see how you are going to."

Rising up, Ursus said, "The way I get my cone seeds is to watch a Chickaree squirrel. He'll climb up and get a mess of them and then bury the seeds for winter storage. Then, I just go dig them up. In fact, I'm really in the mood for some seeds now. Guess I'll head into the forest and see if I can spot a Chickaree squirrel working some cone seeds."

As the huge bear started to depart, Spruce said, "Well, it's been good talking with you. I do hope that we can stay wild and free and the human beings don't invade this place. Good luck."

With a friendly nod, Ursus said, "Same here. And good luck to you, too. I have a hunch that we are both going to need it.

Spruce watched the great bear lumber gracefully across the meadow into the forest. To Spruce, the bear had a dignity and power about him that seemed to enhance the landscape. Spruce watched Ursus' silvery robe rippling over his large and mighty muscles as he gradually disappeared from view. Spruce had learned much from the big bear and had now developed a strong concern about the humans. When would they come to his mountain forest?

(5) THE FOREST RANGERS

The morning after Ursus's visit, Spruce, with a feeling of great concern, watched two people making their way through the forest toward the meadow. As they got closer, he observed that one was taller and younger than the other. Spruce noticed that they were both dressed in brownish clothing with large yellow patches on their shoulders.

As they entered the meadow, Spruce felt a slight shock when the shorter one pointed toward him. With Spruce anxiously watching, they rapidly walked across the meadow towards him. When they arrived, he could see that they were intently studying Ursus's claw marks on his trunk.

The short one, Austin Miller, a district ranger, gazed at the marks. He remembered seeing such high claw marks only twice before in his 26 years with the United States Forest Service. Since being assigned to the Grandview District of Two Moons National Forest in the Northern Rockies eight years ago, Austin had only seen such high claw marks one time. Turning to the taller, female human who was Tommi Wing, his new assistant district ranger, he said, "Now there, Tommi, is the sign of a real big grizzly bear. He'd have to be pretty good sized to put a claw mark up that high.

I was beginning to wonder if there were any of those big bears still around these parts."

Tommi continued to stare at the impressive looking claw marks. Recently graduated with a master's degree from a school of forestry at an eastern university, she had worked for the Forest Service in the South for a short time and was still new to the Western forests. Amazed, Tommi tried to imagine the large and powerful creature behind those awesome marks. She could not believe the fascination she felt to know that such things existed in her assigned district. Recovering from her wonder, she finally said, "Wow! That must be some bear. By the way, those claw marks look awfully fresh. Do you think that it could be in this vicinity?"

Lighting up his pipe, Austin said, "Could be. By the looks of his tracks I'd say that he passed through here over the last day or two. He probably is miles from here by now. But you never know with those darn bears. That's why I always pack my .44 magnum pistol. If it were up to me, I'd clean them out of this country. All they do is cause problems–killing cattle and sheep, ripping up campgrounds–and you heard about the guy who got mauled by a grizzly last summer, didn't you?"

Tommi hesitated before answering. She was thinking about how long these wild and magnificent animals would continue to survive with attitudes like Austin's. Finally, she replied, "Yes, but I also heard that he gave no warning and walked right between a mother grizzly and her cubs. I don't see how we can blame the bear for that accident. Besides, they are an endangered species that need special protection before they become extinct."

Austin studied his new assistant ranger for a moment. He liked the bright young woman who seemed to have a strong love for the outdoors and her job. Yet, he noticed that Tommi would occasionally make remarks like this one that would always take him aback. Austin could not quite place his finger on it. But he knew that Tommi thought differently from himself and most of the other rangers that he had known. Austin wondered about what was going on in forestry schools today when they produced such weird thinking in some of their graduates. In his student days, they taught one how to be a good timber and grazing man without all the wildlife, recreation, and environmental stuff. He made a mental note to get Tommi shaped up for the real world of forest management.

With this, Austin said, "Grizzly bears may be officially classified as a endangered species, but I think that they are very threatening to what we and other people want to do around here. A national forest is for people to use and develop and the bears will simply have to go if there are any conflicts. After all, people pay taxes for the national forest and our salaries. And bears don't. And speaking of our salaries, let's get going on our work on this timber survey to try and earn them. How many board feet do you think we could get out of this nice looking Engelmann spruce right here?"

With a combination of fear and fascination, Spruce watched the forest rangers conduct their study in a very professional way. Tommi stepped back and counted off 16-foot log lengths over her outstretched arm, gradually sighting the length of Spruce. Then she took out a tape and measured Spruce at diameter breast height. After mentally figuring for a few seconds, she turned to Austin and said, "Well, I'd estimate that it would have about 150 board feet. Should be able to get three logs out of it, but beyond that it narrows too much for a full, fourth log." Spruce continued to be fearful, wondering about this strange appraisal by Tommi.

Nodding in agreement, Austin said, "That's exactly what I would have estimated. Now, let me test you a bit on what you learned from your forestry school besides protecting grizzly bears. What are the genus and species names of it?"

Tommi replied, "That's easy. Picea engelmannii. As you probably know, Picea, the Latin genus name, is derived from pix, which means pitch. This genus occurs throughout the north temperate regions of the world and contains a lot of pitch. The species name, Engelmann, was taken from Dr. George Engelmann, a distinguished botanist, whose identifying description of this species of tree first appeared in 1863."

Pleased, Austin remarked, "Sounds like you really know your trees. But now tell me what it's good for."

Tommi replied, "I suppose a lot of things, like watershed protection, food and cover for wildlife, beauty and recreation for people, as well as lumber." Spruce became more and more interested in the conversation as his earlier uncomfortable feelings mixed with a liking for Tommi.

Slightly annoyed, Austin puffed hard on his pipe. As a small cloud of smoke appeared, he remarked, "Look, Tommi, when most foresters are considering the good of a tree, they are usually thinking in terms of harvesting the timber for the uses of its lumber. Surely, your forestry professors taught you about this or didn't they?"

She answered, "They sure did. In fact, that's about all many of them were concerned about–timber management and technical subjects about lumber like forest mensuration, silva culture, and wood technology. I don't believe that some of them will ever realize that the forest is a biological community beyond their lumber and other economic development concerns."

Pausing, Tommi continued, "Sure, I can tell you that Engelmann spruce is one of the lightest of important commercial woods in the United States and it is principally used in home construction and plywood manufacturing with excellent properties for pulp and paper. I know that there is a lot of need and demand in this country for lumber like this despite letting Japan and other countries buy and take so much overseas. Anyway, I'm all for quality timber management and sustainable yield for lumber, but it seems that there is just too much emphasis on it in forestry schools and now in this outfit, particularly under local, economic demands. I think we have to put logging in its proper place along with other values and uses of the forest community. I also think we should leave some forest lands wild and natural without logging. Sorry, I didn't mean to expound, but your point of trees just being good for lumber contrasted with my forestry ideas."

Austin continued to puff harder on his pipe. He was shocked

and embarrassed by his young colleague's attack on the sacred
timber mandate of their agency. Austin now knew that Tommi
would have a lot of problems adjusting to the Forest Service and its
demands for conformity. The agency had easily imposed its values
and policies upon Austin particularly with his desire to please local logging interests. But for Tommi it would be difficult as her
new ideas seemed to spring from deep conviction. Austin regret-
ted that it would be his duty to report Tommi's comments to the
forest supervisor. Yet, he could not help feeling that Tommi, as a
young and idealistic woman, was like a high-spirited young horse
that needed to be broken into a seasoned workhorse like himself.
But Austin did have an intuitive feeling that the Forest Service
needed new blood like Tommi's for healthy and needed changes.
He secretly hoped that Tommi would stick with it, regardless of
problems.

Looking worried, Austin loudly said, "Tommi! Don't you realize that you can get into a lot of trouble with this outfit for making
statements like that?" Furiously, he knocked out his pipe and continued, "You know darn well that we have a job to do out here.
And that timber management is first and foremost. Why do you
think we are out here right now?" Before Tommi could voice a
reply, Austin angrily continued, "Well, I'll tell you right now that
we are not on a nature walk like a couple of dicky birders. We are
on an official assignment with the Forest Service, U.S. Department of Agriculture, to survey the timber resources in this area so
that they can be estimated and contracted to private industry for
logging operations. And that's it!"

Tommi looked her boss squarely in the face and said, "Take it
easy, Austin. I realize that we are out here for that. But we also
have other official responsibilities as well. According to my read-
ings of the agency manuals, one of them happens to be to survey
potential wilderness areas for possible study and classification under the National Wilderness Act of Congress. And this area certainly qualifies in my mind. It has all the wilderness character
needed to. . . ."

Austin interrupted, "1 figured you would get around to that. Well, officially, the forest supervisor has not ordered that any wilderness consideration be given to this area. He and I both agree that the area should be logged as soon as possible. And that's why we're here."

Thinking, Tommi reached out and held one of Spruce's branches. She found the needles to be sharp, firm, and healthy. Releasing them, she commented, "And once this area is logged, it would no longer have any potential for wilderness study, would it, Austin?"

Gradually, Austin's face turned red with embarrassment. He retorted, "That may well be, but there are plenty of local people depending on the logging operations as well as our nation's need for lumber. And . . ."

Tommi interrupted softly, "Austin, you know that this area has high potential for being classified as wilderness. It should be given adequate study as required by Congress before going ahead with any type of logging operations. What is going on, anyway?"

A silence emerged as the two people gazed intently at each other. Tommi thought about Austin's position and tried to understand it. She liked the tough old ranger. But she knew that Austin was thoroughly indoctrinated with timber management philosophy from student days and throughout his career with the Forest Service. In the small towns where Austin had been stationed, he easily merged with the people socially and took on their values and interests. Many of these small towns near national forests, like the community of Big Log where they were stationed, were economically pressed. Yet these same towns had a history of over-exploitation of the surrounding national forest, including clear cutting. There had been too much logging, roading, grazing, and mining on these lands in the past.

Such towns were strong on economic development and exerted considerable pressures on rangers like Austin for more use of the national forest at all costs. Tommi knew that the political and economic leaders of Big Log, including the owners of the three lumber mills, were counted among Austin's friends. Austin served on the Big Log Chamber of Commerce and School Board with them. He played poker with them on Friday nights, and they all had frequent dinners together. In a small-town setting, his wife and children knew their wives and children through school and social activities. The Austins were considered to be a part of the town, including its social and economic problems. And they, in turn, were concerned like the townspeople for the immediate economic interests of Big Log. Yet Big Log would be ruined if it continued to be exploited without sustainable and recreational management.

As Tommi thought about this, she realized that it was difficult to blame the man. Like many rangers, he had simply been conditioned to think in concrete, economic terms for local communities. And the Forest Service administration had encouraged this type of thinking, particularly by having their agency budget tied to logging sales.

Yet Tommi knew that national forests were public lands owned by all of the public, not just the people from nearby towns. The man from Chicago owned a share in a national forest just like the man from Big Log. From studies that she had read, Tommi had observed that most people, particularly those from urban areas, thought of national forests in terms of outdoor recreation and protection of nature. She remembered one study of national public opinion that revealed two out of three Americans favored having plenty of wilderness in national forests. With a tinge of regret, she realized that Austin could simply not think beyond Big Log.

As both rangers became uncomfortable with the long silence, Austin decided to switch the subject. He reached down and plucked some dried, brown leaves from a kinnikinnick plant that was growing along the meadow floor. Most of its leaves were green with bright red berries among then. Both watched as he slowly ground the leaves to particles by rubbing them in his hand. Turning to Tommi, he said, "Did you know that Indians use these leaves for tobacco? Well, actually, they usually mix about half tobacco in half ground up kinnikinnick leaves for a pipeful just like I'm going to do now. It gives a good and mild smoke and flavor." Lighting up his pipe, Austin took several puffs and then offered it to Tommi.

With a smile, Tommi accepted the pipe and also took a few puffs. She handed it back to Austin and said, "That is rather good– very unusual. Say, this is something like an Indian peace pipe ceremony."

Smiling back, Austin commented, "Could be, could be. By the way, did you ever hear the Indian story about kinnikinnick?' Tommi shook her head and Austin continued, "Many moons ago, the kinnikinnick was a small tree with large leaves that fell each fall. It also had brown berries. One winter, a great snow came and flattened all the trees with its clinging weight on their leaves. All the trees with large leaves except kinnikinnick died. When the snow finally melted, kinnikinnick was crushed and pressed upon the ground so that it could not rise up. Yet, still alive, it started to grow by spreading its tiny branches on the ground like a root growth."

Amused, Tommi asked, "It sure doesn't look much like a tree today, does it?"

Austin replied, 'Nope. But the Great Spirit was so glad over kinnikinnick's efforts for survival that he decided to let it live in this new form. He reduced its leaves in size and made them permanently green like the evergreen trees. Then, the Great Spirit changed its berries from brown to red so the birds and squirrels could see its fruit and scatter the seeds in many new places. That's why it's pretty common in the mountains, I guess. By the way, Indians also use this plant as a medicine for colds, coughs, and burns–even for bladder and kidney ailments. It's supposed to be very effective for these things, but I'll stick to using it as a tobacco mixture."

Both rangers felt better after this diversion from their logging and wilderness debate. They resumed their timber survey. As they started to leave the meadow and Spruce, Tommi noticed three hikers making their way toward them. She pointed this out to

Austin who said, "Well, what have we here. Looks like some back-packers getting into this country. Looks like two of them are pretty young. I'll bet the hiking party is that law professor and his two teenagers who wanted to do some camping in this area. Just before leaving, I issued them a fire permit for their trip. They must really like to get into the back country to get way up here like this. Sometimes, I have a hard time figuring out people who like to do this type of thing just for fun."

Tommi commented, "One thing for sure is that we will be seeing a lot more wilderness visitors like them. My forest recreation courses all indicated that there are sharp increases in outdoor recreation like this. I guess it represents a strong need on the part of a lot of people for wild and natural country and for getting away from the pressures of civilization. What do you think?"

Austin answered, 'Well, I do know that I'm seeing more and more of this kind of people over the years–maybe too many to keep track of. But we just can't lock up any area like this for some of the public to enjoy. After all, there are plenty of other people and uses to be considered from logging to motorized recreation. And now we have those All Terrain Vehicles or ATVs that can go anywhere. Some people have a lot of fun with them–tearing around the countryside."

Austin stopped talking as the hiking party approached within hearing distance. Both rangers could not help admiring the two young people as they hiked so energetically with their backpacks. As Austin had predicted, the party was the law professor and his two teenagers. After a brief visit with the backpackers, the forest rangers departed to carry on their timber survey.

(6) THE HIKING PARTY

Surprised and fascinated with all the human activity, Spruce had intently observed the visit between the forest rangers and the hiking party. Spruce learned from their conversations that they now knew the forest rangers were making a timber survey for logging and noticed the looks of shock and dismay that had appeared on the faces of the newcomers. The word "wilderness" was mentioned several times by the backpackers before the rangers departed.

As the rangers disappeared from view, Heather Spur turned to her father and said, "Dad, does this mean that they are going to log this wonderful place–even that beautiful spruce tree over there?"

Her brother Paul picked up where Heather left off, " Dad, I think that this is the best spot that we have ever been in. They just can't go ahead and rip it up with logging and roads can they?"

Professor Frank Spur studied his concerned teenagers for a few moments before replying. As far back as he could remember, both had radiated a love and concern for nature in all its forms. True, he had done his best to provide plenty of outdoor experiences as his father had done for him. But, somehow, these two had a natural awareness and a healthy idealism for protecting nature that even went beyond his understanding. Their questions of concern were very typical of them.

Finally he answered, "Now, hold on you two! Nothing has been done yet beyond the timber survey that we just heard about. And we all did make the point to the rangers that the area should be studied for wilderness first, didn't we?"

Heather replied, "Yes, Dad, but that older forest ranger sure didn't seem to like it. In fact, I thought I saw him turn a little red—like we said a naughty word or something."

Paul commented, "That's right, but I also noticed that the other ranger was almost smiling then."

Professor Spur said, "Be that as it may, the Forest Service will definitely have to look into the wilderness possibilities for this area. It certainly rates high in my book so far. But to get to more practical topics, where are we going to set up our campsite, folks?"

Heather answered, "How about right here, Dad? From this meadow overlook we have a tremendous view and I just love that spruce tree with the bear claws on it. I've never seen such a magnificent and gorgeous tree. It seems like a symbol of the wilderness around here. Let's just camp right here. We can get our water from that little stream just below."

Paul said, "It's fine with me too—so that makes two votes. But what about those claw marks on the tree? They sure look fresh. Do you think a grizzly bear might be around?"

Professor Spur laughed and said, "Are you kidding? With the chatter from you characters—not to mention our bear bells that have been ringing all the way up here—I'm told that they make a noise louder than an ambulance siren to a bear's delicate hearing. I'm sure that we won't have to worry about any grizzly around here. C'mon, let's get our camp set up."

Spruce watched as the hiking party rapidly began to dismantle equipment from their backpacks. Although they looked a bit tired from hiking, He noticed that everyone pitched in without complaining. In no time, there appeared a strange dwelling that they called a tent and they placed sleeping bags inside. Spruce saw other objects being placed here and there in what appeared to be a well-organized campsite. At first, he became startled at the sight of a small fire flaming up near the tent, but everything looked under control and comfortable.

As Professor Spur threw a log on the campfire, he said, "This is great! Too bad that your mother can't be here with us. I wish she did not have to take that required course for her master's degree this summer. But at least she can be with us next summer when we come up here again. Right, gang?"

Paul answered, "I sure hope so, particularly if those forest rangers don't arrange to have a logging company in here by then."

Professor Spur commented, "That still bugging you? I still think there may not be that much to worry about, particularly with a wilderness study of this area. And . . ."

Heather interrupted, 'But, Dad, Paul may be right. After all, the rangers were in here doing a timber survey and not a wilderness study. And I'm sure a lot of logging companies would like to get in here as soon as they can. Gosh, I just could not bear it if they cut down that beautiful spruce tree over there."

Heather grabbed the canvas water bucket and started toward the small stream. On the way, she paused near Spruce and reached out to touch one of his branches. Heather had felt a communion of spirit with Spruce since she had arrived in the meadow. Somehow she noticed a certain radiance from it and felt the sensitivity and innocence of the tree that was much like her own free spirit. Heather wondered about the tree and its possible feelings, emotions, and personality. Somehow, she felt Spruce liked her and wanted to express his concern to her about the logging. Heather wished with all her heart that she could talk to this magnificent tree.

Finally, Heather whispered, "Don't worry my spruce tree in the wilderness. We will make sure that no one cuts you down. I promise!" Amazed, she felt–or perhaps thought she felt–some type of response of relief that came from Spruce. Continuing on her way to the stream, Heather reflected on this feeling. She remembered reading some controversial research about plants responding to human emotions. In several experiments that she had read, scientists had hooked up lie detectors to plants which recorded their apparent responses to love and fear. She recalled one experiment that made the lie detector attached to the plants soar when a man who had the thought of killing one of them came into the room. Yet the plants failed to respond when other people entered.

Heather remembered an experiment that she performed herself. It had been based on an experiment she had read about and decided to duplicate. She had taken two young, potted plants and given them equal sunlight and water. But she gave one of the plants a great deal of love and attention and talked to it a lot. The other plant was completely ignored beyond providing for its physical requirements. In several weeks, Heather noticed that the plant getting the attention was over a third larger than the neglected plant. The attention plant was thriving and radiant. She then believed that her love and attention had a definite effect on the plant. Heather thought that this type of thing must have something to do with her early rapport with Spruce.

Heather finally reached the stream and began to fill the canvas bucket. Still thinking about the spruce, she felt closer to the mysteries of nature. There were many things that could not yet be explained with scientific or practical intelligence, and she found this to be particularly true in a wild and natural area like this one.

Heather had read somewhere that wilderness contained the answers to questions that were not even formulated at this time. "Someday," she thought to herself, "maybe I'll be an ecologist and study the ecology of wilderness. I could study the complicated relations between plants and animals without having to worry about all the artificial effects of people, including logging and roads—and those horrible ATVs." Yet she knew that she would never know all of the wonders and mysteries of nature, like her feeling of friendship and communion with Spruce. Some things simply had to be accepted as beyond her comprehension and understanding. With these thoughts in mind, Heather started back toward camp.

When she arrived, Paul asked, "Hey, where have you been? We were beginning to wonder where you were."

Heather answered, "Oh just getting the water and thinking, I guess."

Professor Spur commented, "Well, a wilderness experience like this does provide stimulation and inspiration for deep thought and creativity. I get some of my best ideas for my teaching and research out here. I guess it is just a response to the natural influences. Penny for your thoughts, Heather."

Starting to help with getting dinner ready, Heather said, "I'd rather not talk about them now. By the way, Dad, this stew sure smells good. When will it be ready? I'm starved!"

Professor Spur replied, "Pretty soon, I guess. For tomorrow, we'll try and get some nice trout for our frying pan."

Paul said, "That sounds great! But right now, I'm hungry as a bear for that stew. Can we eat as soon as I warm up these rolls, Dad?"

Shaking his head in amazement, Professor Spur said, "I can't see how you guys can be that hungry after a big lunch and then polishing off about a pound of trail-mix. With all those raisins, peanuts, chocolates, and whatnot in it, one would think that you both had enough stored energy for a week."

With the hot rolls ready, the stew quickly disappeared as the campers turned to the boiled, dried apricots for dessert. After washing dishes, they sipped hot chocolate while watching the disappearing sunset. Their campfire was like a red, orange flower, blossoming and flickering in the darkening night. In its enchanting, magic-like glow, Spruce appeared like a silent, sculptured statue. The hikers felt very close and at peace as they gazed into the mysterious campfire that seemed to cast a quiet, primitive spell over them.

Breaking the silence, Paul said, "Boy, I feel like some kind of an Indian or frontiersman by a campfire a long time ago. Just sort of natural and free, yet secure."

His father commented, "I know what you mean, son. Campfires have been a blessing to mankind for centuries upon centuries and this one is a thread of that primitive past. Guess it sort of links us all together."

Throwing another log on the fire, Heather said, "Well, among other things, I sure appreciate its being nice and warm. Hey, let's break out some of those marshmallows and toast them." With nods of agreement, the hikers were soon munching hot, melted marshmallows on short sticks after holding them over the fire.

When they had all settled back again and relaxed, Paul said, "Dad, I'm still worried that they may log this place."

Heather added, "Me too, Dad, and I did make a promise to that beautiful spruce tree that I would not let that happen."

Professor Spur saw the concern on their faces and thought for a moment before replying, "O.K., if it's bugging you guys that much, we'll check with those forest rangers again when we get out. We can stop at their district headquarters in Big Log. But this will mean that we will have to leave a day earlier. How do you feel about that?"

Paul and Heather both nodded affirmatively. Then Paul asked, "But Dad, if this doesn't do any good—you know—if they stall us off about the wilderness study or something—could we contact Congressman Sam Nelson about it? You were friends in college together and still write to each other. I'll bet he'd look into this for you if you asked him to."

His father answered, "I'm sure that he would do it. Sam is very responsible in responding to requests from his constituents and he also happens to be a back packer himself. Tell you what—if there are problems with the forest rangers, how about you guys writing him for help?" Heather and Paul looked at each other and nodded in agreement.

Heather poured herself another cup of hot chocolate and said, "Another thing we ought to do is come up with some reasons why wilderness is important for the public. That way we can have some arguments for saving this place as wilderness. After all, national forests like this are public lands. And the public does own them and does have the right to do what it wants with them, not just what the logging companies, ATVs, miners, or the Forest Service want."

Professor Spur agreed, "Good idea! how about making some kind of a game of coming up with what Heather said. We can all take turns at coming up with some wilderness values for the public. So we won't lose this ammunition in case we need it–I'll volunteer to write down some of the main points. O.K., who will be first?"

Paul replied, "I'll take a stab at it. How about personal achievement? It seems like so many activities today are either too structured or make you into a spectator. When I get out here in the wilderness, I know I really have to make it as an individual on my own under rugged conditions. It's really healthy exercise with challenges. I've gained a lot of self-respect by having the persistence and fortitude for it. I really enjoy the feeling of making it to where we are going as well as getting there. Guess I sort of feel a spirit of the struggle similar to the individual from early frontier days from wilderness hiking."

Heather added, "And there are also social values of that, too. I know we share mutual respect and cooperation together by being out here in the wilderness as a family–sort of an *esprit de corps*. In fact, I've never felt so close to you both than when we are out here in the wilderness together as a family. I guess its because we are all sharing the same wilderness experiences of natural beauty, serenity, and hardships. Speaking of hardships, I won't ask you to share this mean, old blister on my ankle. Anyway, wilderness and you guys–too bad Mom isn't here–make for a unique social experience. Just like right now around this campfire. I know that we have never had such closeness and great conversations at home, particularly with all the activities and TV."

Professor Spur smiled and said, "You're right, Heather. I know that we all get too involved with activities and pressures for that matter. In fact, one thing that I would like to suggest is the psychological stress relief of being in the wilderness. The general complications and tempo of our modern lives disturb our peace of mind with too much stress. Wilderness provides us with an important antidote that relieves or prevents stress through the healing of natural surroundings. When I get up here in the mountains and forest, for example, I feel like I am in another world. All the things that were bugging me seem to vanish."

Paul added, "Me too, Dad–even that low grade I got from Mr. McDougal, my algebra teacher."

Heather commented, "I wonder if it is because, through wilderness, we realize how small we are in the natural scheme of things. It sort of gives us a perspective to realize our natural beginnings and just how small our problems really are."

Paul said, "I'd buy that. And I think a lot of this comes from our trying to understand and appreciate the things around us, like that spruce tree. I guess we get a sense of humility and closeness to real life from them. But, you know, Heather, if Mom were here, I'm sure she would right away say nature appreciation. She just loves to study and photograph the plant and animal life in a wilderness."

Professor Spur said, "And I can testify to all the rolls of film that she goes through. I guess that we all appreciate seeing the undisturbed plants and animals here. They remain and evolve in their natural state as they have for centuries. Guess it is something like entering a natural world or living museum. I think anyone would be thrilled by seeing the wildlife and unspoiled beauty of primeval forests around here. Yet, there are some people who do not recognize intangible values like these. They prefer short term, economic, and exploitive values or interests in contrast to long term, intangible, and qualitative values that we are trying to identify and describe. Yet I know that most Americans really look at their National Forests for the latter values and want to leave behind the idea of a frontier exploitive view toward unlimited resources.

Spruce listened intently as the hiking party continued to play their game of wilderness values for another hour until they finally

crawled into their sleeping bags for some rest. Through the glow
of the campfire, Spruce watched Professor Spur diligently taking
notes on their conversations. To the list they had added wilderness
values dealing with the spiritual, quality recreation, fishing and
hunting, biodiversity, creativity, watershed, and history. Spruce
could not help but reflect that many of the values seemed to say
that the living things of the wilderness had a right to live out their
lives for their own sake in an undisturbed way—to carry on their
struggle for survival without interference from people.

Spruce took great comfort in hearing such values from these
human beings.

After breakfast the next day, the hiking party got ready for a
fishing expedition. During a careful examination of his fly collec-
tion, Paul paused suddenly, and said, "Dad, one value that we
forgot to mention last night was future generations. After all, when
we are gone, there will be plenty of people in the future who will
want some wilderness around. We should see that they at least
have an equal opportunity to seek the satisfactions in wilderness
that we do." Professor Spur got out his notebook and proudly
wrote down his son's thoughts.

Agreeing, Heather commented, "Good point. I wonder if our
great-grandchildren will ever have the opportunities that we do
now. With all the pressures to develop everything in this country,
it seems only fair that future generations should have these wilderness opportunities. And I think that we have responsibilities to see
to this heritage so we can be good ancestors."

Grabbing his fly rod, Professor Spur said, "O.K., I have that
officially recorded. Now, let's go fishing."

When the hiking party returned in the late afternoon, Spruce
noticed that they had a nice mess of cutthroat trout with them. In
no time, they had the trout cleaned and in the frying pan after
covering them with butter and bread crumbs. They ate them along
with generous portions of fried potatoes and onions. For three more
days, the hiking party remained camped in the meadow near Spruce
while going on sojourns into the surrounding countryside. The

next morning there was a great deal of activity as they proceeded to break camp. Spruce would miss them.

Just before they departed, Heather walked over and said, "My Spruce in the wilderness, how we enjoyed camping by you! I'll do my very best to keep my promise to you. Guess we have to go now. Goodbye for now."

(7) CITIZEN ACTION

For the rest of the summer Spruce continued to live and grow as before, little knowing how the future was to depend upon something foreign and unknown to him—politics.

When the hiking party arrived in Big Log, they immediately proceeded to the district headquarters of the Forest Service. They found Austin chatting amicably with Mr. Quincy Sawyer, one the owners of a local sawmill, over a cup of coffee. After introducing them to Mr. Sawyer, Austin asked, "Well, did you people have a good time in the back country?"

Professor Spur replied, "Sure did. Certainly great wilderness country up there. By the way, we were rather concerned about your timber survey and wondered what your plans are for the area? I am sure that it would more than qualify for a wilderness study and classification."

Austin and Mr. Sawyer exchanged quick glances. Then Austin answered, "There are no plans for a wilderness at this time. As I see it . . ."

Mr. Sawyer interrupted, "And there better not be in the future! Others and myself are in the process of placing bids with the Forest Service on timber sales up in that area right now. Why the whole economy of Big Log is tied up in our getting plenty of timber for our lumber mills here, not to mention the need for lumber by the rest of the country. We don't want any wilderness stuff tying up all that good timber up there."

Austin turned red with embarrassment as he listened to Mr. Sawyer expound. He secretly wished that the hikers had not come into his office when his logging friend was there. Austin hated controversies like this.

When Mr. Sawyer stopped talking, Professor Spur turned to Austin and said, "And I suppose that you also have logging roads planned for the area?" Lighting up his pipe and puffing rapidly, Austin replied, "Well, in our planning process, we did designate some potential sites for logging roads, but this is a normal part of our management planning."

Pointing to the large map of the ranger district on the wall, Professor Spur asked, "Would you mind pointing out some of them on the map?"

Austin hesitated and finally answered, "I do not believe that it is exactly appropriate to discuss our management planning with the public at this initial stage."

Paul exclaimed, "But I will bet Mr. Sawyer knows about them if he wants to get the lumber up there. Isn't he a member of the public like we are?"

Mr. Sawyer shifted uncomfortably as Austin replied, "Well, son, that is in the category of a business transaction with the Forest Service. After all, Mr. Sawyer and others in the lumber industry do make their living through arrangements like this and . . ."

Professor Spur interrupted, "But, under the Freedom of Information Act, I am sure that we are also entitled to this public information. In fact, as a lawyer, I know that we have a right to this information right now."

Turning bright red, Austin walked over to the map and traced out several of the proposed routes for the designated logging roads.

Heather shouted, "Daddy, that one road goes right through the place that we just came through! Why, it would probably go through the meadow where my spruce tree is. I don't like this at all."

Mr. Sawyer said, "Look here, how else are we going to get the logs out of there? There's valuable timber up there and we are going to get it out. The trees will come back in time and people can use the logging roads later for motorized recreation. In fact, a lot more people will be able to get up there on the logging roads. I don't see why you people are so concerned about what we are trying to do."

Professor Spur firmly said, "We are talking about lands that the public owns. As a wilderness, the area may just be a lot more valuable to the public than the lumber and profits you can get from it at the cost to taxpayers of subsidizing and building those roads. And this is also why we want a wilderness study done on it before anything further takes place. We all know that logging it before the study would automatically disqualify it for wilderness. What about it, Ranger? Are we going to have a wilderness study or not before the logging takes place?"

Austin answered, 'Like I said, I really cannot say at this time. Maybe you ought to get in touch with the supervisor of Two Moon National Forest. I can give you his address and telephone number." With this, the hiking party took their leave.

After leaving the district office, Professor Spur placed a long-distance call to the national forest supervisor. In response to inquiries about the wilderness study, the forest supervisor was cordial, but noncommittal. Professor Spur felt frustrated when he reported the results of his call to Heather and Paul.

Then Heather suggested, "Dad, let's stay overnight in Big Log. We would have the rest of the day to learn about what might be happening to the forest that way."

Professor Spur agreed, "O.K., but we have to leave for home early tomorrow. I have to attend a faculty meeting."

The hiking party found Big Log humming with excitement. There was a great deal of talk about large timber sales that were to be made by the Forest Service. When they dropped into the Chamber of Commerce, the executive director told them, "This town is really going to prosper with those big timber sales. We even have out-of-state lumber and mining companies that are planning to locate here as a result. And we have been contacted by a lot of motorized vehicle groups which include ATVs, and Snowmobilers who can also use the roads to get in there. It's about time they really opened up the forest so we can use it like it should be used. This is the greatest thing that's ever happened to Big Log."

When they asked when the logging would start, he replied, "Oh, I figure in less than a month according to what I've heard from my friends with the Forest Service and lumber companies. They claim the bulldozers will be arriving soon so they can start roughing out the logging roads."

Getting more and more alarmed and discouraged, the hiking party found that this information and sentiment was shared by many of the Big Log people whom they talked to. Yet they found some who seriously questioned the move. A sporting goods store owner said, "They don't have to do something like this on such a large scale. It's going to ruin the watershed and hurt quality recreation around here. And when they cut down those big trees and forests–heard it takes over two hundred years for them to come back–I'll never see anything like them in my lifetime again. Nope, it is just not right. But try and tell some of these dollar-hungry people around here that."

At a drugstore, a minister said, "I don't like it anymore than you do. Those majestic, silent forests provide the solitude and tranquility where people can feel close to God. I hike up there often to get my spiritual batteries recharged. It will be very sad to see them destroyed. But that's what they're going to do, regardless." The minister also pointed out the "We Support the Timber Industry" signs in some of the stores and noted that the store managers had plenty of pressure put on them to have the signs in their windows.

On the way back to University City early the next morning,

Heather said, "Dad, guess that now is the time to get in touch with Congressman Nelson, right?"

Paul said, "It sure is . And we had better move fast with those bulldozers supposed to arrive any day to make the logging roads. They really want to get the area developed fast so it will not have a chance as wilderness.

Professor Spur replied, "Right. In fact, we had better send an e-mail with the request that Congressman Sam Nelson immediately look into the situation. We can then write a long letter that explains everything in detail. How does that sound?"

Heather said, 'Great! But what do you think he will do about it?"

Professor Spur replied, "I don't know, but Sam is a very smart man and his heart is in the right place. However, one thing that we will have to worry about is backing him up with plenty of information, reasons, and citizen support."

Paul said, "Well, one thing that we can use will be those wilderness ideas and values that we hammered out that night over the campfire. We'll have to get out those notes that you made, Dad. Also, we can all write up our impressions of the area from our trip there. That would supply some wilderness information for Congressman Nelson."

Professor Spur nodded with approval and said, "Those things should help a lot, but we will have to be prepared for a lot of rebuttal from the Forest Service and the logging companies. I'm sure that they have been collecting a lot of facts and details to support their position. And, don't forget, they have been there a long time so they know it a lot better than we do on our short trip."

Heather asked, "Dad, do you mean to say that whether there will be wilderness or logging will depend on the number of facts and details that either side gets?"

Professor Spur liked the question and mulled it over for a few moments. Finally, he replied, "Not exactly, but having a lot of facts and details certainly makes for a strong case. Maybe I'm looking at it too much from my background as a lawyer, but it seems . . ."

Heather interrupted, "But, Dad, that's not fair. The Forest Service and lumber companies have all kinds of time to collect stuff like that and we don't. I agree we can get some information on it, but I'm sure that it will not even be a fraction of what they get, particularly working together like they do. It's unfair!"

Paul added, "That's right, Dad. We can't come up with very much from University City in less than a month."

Playing the devil's advocate, Professor Spur warmed up to questioning his daughter and son. He asked, "O.K., but how else are politicians and officials supposed to make decisions on things like this?"

Heather defiantly replied, "On what's good for the public–on what the public values for its own public lands."

Paul joined, "Right on, Heather! The way it is now all we have is the forest rangers and lumber companies deciding what they want to do and then going ahead to collect a lot of stuff to support their position. They keep it like a closed system. It should really be an open system with the public and its values involved."

Professor Spur offered a challenge, "Wait a minute, you guys. Forest rangers are professionally trained in forestry. Why can't they decide what is best for the forest and the public?"

Paul answered, "Dad, from what little I know from our visits to rangers and national forests, I just don't think that they can. They just to want to use and develop everything in the forest–like that ranger at Big Log. Seems like they just can't stand to let things alone and natural and wild. Yet they want to economically use and manage everything for loggers and developers in their local towns, including those motorized recreation people. And that's why most of them don't like wilderness, I think."

Heather added, "After all, they are just human beings like the rest of us, and we are all equal when it comes to value decisions like this. I feel that we have just as much a right as they do when it comes to deciding whether or not a beautiful area should be logged or not. It is basically a value decision—what we believe as individuals. I am not going to sit back and let some ranger decide to cut down Spruce and the other trees up there. After all, I own a share of that national forest—just like the rest of the public and the forest ranger.

Smiling, Professor Spur said, 'All right, I surrender. I must admit that much of this comes down to values like you said, Heather. What people believe is right and worthwhile will make up the values that they want for something. In this case, it's logging and roading values against wilderness values and we have got to get our values out to where they can be effective in politics. And that means getting to the public and Congressman Nelson."

Paul asked, 'Dad, do you think that a lot of people feel the same way we do about wilderness?"

Professor Spur answered, "Yes, I do. A recent nationwide survey of the public revealed that more than two out of three Americans favored preservation of national forests over increased timber harvesting."

Heather commented, "Still, it's so hard to get people involved today. My civics teacher, Mr. Burns, said the American public is pretty apathetic about almost everything."

Professor Spur said, "Well, that may be true in a lot of cases, but most people will respond when they can relate something to their personal values. Did I ever tell you about this colleague of mine, a shy and retiring zoology professor, who became an environmental activist?"

As Paul and Heather shook their heads no, Professor Spur continued. "Well, Dr. Leslee was doing research on a very rare lizard in California. As far as he knew, his small study area in the desert was the last habitat for this species. He told the county commissioners about it, and they promised not to develop the area. Then he got a grant to do research in Hawaii for a year. When he returned, he found a shopping center and motel right in the middle of the study area.

Paul asked, "What did he do then."

Professor Spur replied, "What could he do? He was shocked with the knowledge that the small, desert habitat was ruined. He could not find any traces of the rare lizard anywhere in the vicinity. Dr. Leslee angrily protested to the county commissioners who conveniently did not have any record of his request for protecting the area. Somehow, this tragic experience completely transformed the man. Last I heard, he was working with the Nature Conservancy to protect and purchase natural areas before they are developed. And he is a real fighter. He will take on any public or private official who tries to stop public efforts for a natural area and expose the weak points in their positions while letting the public know what is happening.

"I think it was just a case of his real values emerging when he became angry enough at negative and destructive actions toward nature. In the same way, I think a lot of the public will respond to protect wilderness when they see it and their values for it being threatened. They just may need to get a little mad so their values will emerge to protect it. Sometimes, I think young people like you are more sensitive to this type of thing than we older folks are when it comes to responding to protecting nature."

Paul asked, "Say, Heather, do you recall that true story about the children and Olympic National Park that Mr. Burns, your biology teacher, told you?"

Heather answered, "Sure, back in the 1930's, the logging companies were cutting down all of the virgin forests on the Olympic Peninsula of the state of Washington. They were getting into this very scenic and unique area of mountains and old growth forests. Some children from Seattle and places nearby did not want to see it ruined and were very concerned. So they started writing letters to President Franklin Roosevelt about saving it. Kids from all over the country heard about it and also started writing letters, too. Finally, President Roosevelt declared it a National Park as a result of all the letters from children. And it has been protected as designated wilderness since that time. I guess you could call it kid power."

Professor Spur commented, "See, that proves that it can be

done, particularly by young people like you. Hey, we're starting to come up on University City."

When the hiking party reached home and resumed their normal activities, almost all of their spare time over the month was devoted to a flurry of efforts to get the wilderness study. An email was sent right away to Congressman Nelson with a detailed letter from Heather and Paul soon after. Several days passed. Then the administrative assistant for the Congressman called and said they were giving immediate attention to the matter.

In the meantime, Heather and Paul gave short talks on the Grandview area and why it should be classified as a wilderness. Whenever possible, they would use color-slides to illustrate some of the beauty and uniqueness of it. Heather even had two slides that portrayed Spruce's beauty and splendor. They would always conclude their talks with an urgent request for the audience to write to their Congressmen, especially to Representative Nelson. They made their presentations at meetings of high school clubs, church groups, nature organizations, outdoor clubs, environmental organizations.

At the University, Professor Spur was very active in bringing the wilderness matter before his colleagues. He pointed out that the wilderness qualities of the area were valuable to the university for research, education, and recreation. He gave talks at meetings of many social organizations in University City like the Kiwanis, Lions Club, student and faculty clubs, and alumni organizations.

At one meeting, an editor of a newspaper asked if one of his reporters could do a story on it. Professor Spur arranged to have the reporter drop in at home when Heather and Paul were there. They gave their presentation to the reporter that afternoon. It appeared in the morning's newspapers with the caption, "Hiking Family Tries to Save Wilderness from Logging."

The next day they were interviewed on TV and again, as many times before, they made their urgent plea for people to write to their Congressmen.

Four days later, Congressman Nelson called Professor Spur and said, "My God, Frank, you really know how to put the pressure on Congress. My office alone has received more than two thousand letters on this wilderness study, not to mention hundreds of emails and telephone calls. The state's entire Congressional delegation has been swamped with communications from home on this matter. By the way, a lot of the writers are young people and refer to your kids calling it to their attention. Some of them even wrote to the President of the United States. I just can't get over it. Really gave me strong public backing for the action I'm taking."

Professor Spur asked, "What are you going to do, Sam?"

Congressman Nelson replied, "Well, Frank, I got the Forest Service to declare a moratorium on logging and the building of logging roads until we can take a look at the area. I sent one of my staff to Big Log, and he called back right away to tell me that the bulldozers were already beginning to carve roads up there. Fortunately, the moratorium just stopped them before they really got started. All I got from the Forest Service was that they were proceeding with their original management plan. But they finally said they would hold off temporarily under the outside public pressure and my insistence. Now, I am proceeding with my own plan to hold a public hearing on its wilderness study and classification. I am also organizing a Congressional field trip to the area with two other Congressmen. So there will be plenty of action on starting to move it toward wilderness study–thanks to the public interest generated by you people."

Professor Spur was elated as he exclaimed, "Great Sam! I knew that you'd be able to do something on this if anybody could. I can't wait to tell Heather and Paul. And . . ."

Sam interrupted, "Frank, it's still going to be a very rough battle with a lot of opposition. For example, Congressman Wagner McPloiter has insisted on coming along with me on the field trip and public hearing. He is definitely opposed to wilderness and is backed by the lumber and mining industries. He gets a big hunk of his campaign finances from them, not to mention motorized recreation of "Multiple Use" groups which, in turn, get a lot of their money from Japanese and American motor corporations. This guy is going to be a tough cookie to deal with. Anyway, it will sure be good to get out in the wilderness again myself. The descriptions and values of the area by you and your kids sound tremendous. As a matter of fact they sound like there is really a chance to qualify under the Federal Wilderness Act. I'll be in touch shortly. Bye, Frank."

(8) THE CONGRESSIONAL FIELD TRIP

In the early fall after the hiking party's visit, Spruce observed a group of five people approaching the meadow. They were riding on top of strange animals that were larger than elk. Spruce could make out Austin's face as they entered the meadow. Then came the surprise and joy of seeing Heather riding behind on a large white and brown animal. Then she got off it and ran to Spruce.

As Heather ran across the meadow, she was thrilled to see her favorite tree and to be in the wilderness again. Because of the growing state and national attention on the Grandview area generated by the Spurs, Congressman Nelson had asked them to join him on the field trip. But Professor Spur had too heavy a teaching schedule at the university to leave, and Paul was on the high school football team with the homecoming game coming up. In absolute delight at the invitation to join a Congressional field trip to the back country, Heather had accepted with the blessings of her family and teachers. In fact, Mr. Burns, her civics teacher, told her, "You'll probably learn more about Congress in one week out there than I can teach you in a semester in a classroom."

Looking back to see that the party was out of hearing distance, Heather finally reached Spruce and said, "See, my beautiful Spruce in the wilderness, I came back and we are doing our very best to see that you and this place stay wild and free. A lot of people want this now, and I just hope we can talk Congress and the government into it."

Nodding toward the other people, Heather continued, "See that tall man with the sideburns, Spruce. He is Congressman Sam Nelson, and he's our friend who is trying to get something done about it. That short, fat man is Congressman Wagner McPloiter. I just don't like him. He seems like a selfish person to me, and he's already made some bad remarks about wilderness. I'm not sure about the other one, Congressman Vince Middleberry–the one with the mustache. He just doesn't seem to have much character–hard to figure out him out.

Fondly holding one of Spruce's branches, Heather went on, "And then there's Austin, the forest ranger who was up here before. He's been extra nice and friendly to everyone. I guess he is supposed to be our guide on the field trip. We can only stay here one night since Austin wants to take us all over the place to different spots. Gee, my wilderness Spruce, you look so great and magnificent. Did you know that I showed slides of you to hundreds of people?"

Forgetting everything else, Heather went on enthusiastically to tell Spruce about all the activities of the Spurs in trying to save the Grandview area. Suddenly, she felt the presence of someone near her. Looking around, she saw Congressman Nelson standing quietly with a friendly smile on his face. Startled, Heather exclaimed, "Gee, I hope that you don't think I'm some kind of nut– talking to a tree like this!"

Congressman Nelson warmly replied, "Nope, not a bit, Heather. I do myself sometimes when I'm alone in the forest. Incidentally, I can sense a special relationship between you and that magnificent spruce. Wow, what a big grizzly bear that must have been–to make claw marks on it like that. Anyway, I'm sorry to

intrude, but I did want to talk to you alone for a moment. As you
know, we will be holding a public hearing in Big Log on the wilderness potential of this area when we finish our field trip. A great
deal depends on the impressions and comments that we Congressmen can take back to the Public Lands Committee of Congress.
Understand?"

Heather nodded as Congressman Nelson continued, "By now,
I'm sure you know where Congressman McPloiter stands. With
his backing by lumber, mining and motorized recreation industries, he has opposed or tried to sabotage about every wilderness
proposal coming before Congress. But Congressman Middleberry
has really not come out on either side of wilderness issues. He is a
compromising, but very astute politician–and I might add a very
influential member of the Public Lands Committee."

Heather observed, "He certainly is a quiet man and doesn't
seem to have very much personality."

Congressman Nelson laughed and said, "A lot of people get
that first impression, but he is a very sensitive and intelligent man
with a lot of depth. This is his first real experience of actually
being out in a wilderness. I'm surprised that he wanted to come,
but he said something about needing to get away for a while. At
any rate, a lot of our hopes rest on what he does on the committee.
So do what you can to get him headed in the right direction."

Glancing at Spruce, Heather said, "I sure will. I will also make
it a point to tell him about those wilderness values that Dad, Paul,
and I hammered out right here. We better get back and help the
others set up camp.

Austin, who was very organized, soon had a comfortable campsite established with everyone pitching in. A modest campfire was
soon sizzling thick T-bone steaks on a grill. With strong appetites
from their day outdoors, the party quickly polished off the steaks
along with generous helpings of salad and baked potatoes. This
was followed by hot coffee and sliced peaches. As they lounged
around the campfire full and contented, Congressman Middleberry

remarked, "I can't remember when a dinner was so delicious as this one–even in the best restaurants in the Capital."

Bursting with pride, Austin said, 'Shucks, Congressman Middleberry, just being outdoors makes most food taste pretty good."

Congressman Nelson suggested, "As long as we're out here for a week, let's call each other by first names. I think that everyone feels less formal in the back country than anywhere else. Sort of a natural bond of common humanity in nature rather than all the roles we play outside. How about it?"

Everyone in the party quickly agreed.

Then Congressman McPloiter said, "Sure, we're all equal. After all, that's one of the principles our great country was founded on. But are we all equal when it comes to getting out here in back country like this? It seems to me that only the wealthy, leisure class can afford to use wilderness. We can't go on setting aside public lands for a few rich people who have the money and time to get here. What about all the public with low incomes who can't afford the costs? That is certainly not being very equal in my mind."

With a wry grin, Sam responded, "Wagner, there has been plenty of research showing that the costs associated with wilderness recreation are much lower than those associated with other types of recreation. The studies show that wilderness recreation is a matter of individual preference, regardless of income and leisure time available. And let's face it, a camper pickup, a snowmobile, 4- wheel drive vehicle or ATV will cost a lot more than a backpack and tent or a good pack horse."

Heather added, "That's right, Sam. The wilderness visitors that I've seen are a cross-section of Americans with young, middle-aged, or old and are poor, middle class and rich in income. The things they have in common are their efforts to get there and their appreciation for wilderness values."

Wagner lit up a long cigar and puffed for a moment while thinking. Then he said, "Still, there are too few people using places like this. If we had roads up here, than a lot more people could be up here enjoying themselves."

Sam responded, "But then it could no longer be considered wilderness and its unique values would be destroyed. That's why the Wilderness Act, as you know, prohibits permanent development like roads as well as motorized vehicles. Can you imagine what would happen to the quiet and wild atmosphere of this place with camper trailers, ATVs, and thousands of people driving around?"

Blowing clouds of smoke into the night air, Wagner casually replied, "Well, I wouldn't mind. Besides, we can't afford to lock up the timber resources in this area. Austin told me that the Big Log community needs that timber badly for its economy."

Sam offered, "I did some homework on that and found that they are now cutting at less than two-thirds of the potential timber available in other parts of Two Moon National Forest lands. I believe there is pressure to get these big or old growth trees as easy pickings for logging."

Wagner retorted, "but they are certainly susceptible to forest fires and insect attacks. Then no one would get any use from them. So they might as well be logged. Austin, tell them about that experience that you told me about earlier today."

Austin quickly responded, "When I was a ranger in the Umpahgre National Forest in Colorado, I witnessed thousands of acres of large Engelmann spruce killed by the spruce budworm. They had built up to an epidemic population through a favorable and small area of damaged Engelmann spruce as a result of lightning storms. The massive populations of beetles and their larvae then attacked the Engelmann spruce in the rest of the forest by tunneling into their cambium layer. That caused the ultimate death of the trees. The undeveloped forest made it difficult to get back there and control epidemics like this. And the same applies to forest fires. Without roads, forests are difficult to manage when it comes to problems like this."

Sam was going around filling the cups of the party with hot

coffee from the pot over the campfire. Settling back again, he said, "That may be, Austin. But you know that healthy trees can resist the beetle if they are not swamped with the attack of a massive population of them. It would not have been too difficult to get in there and control that small area of damaged trees before the epidemic started through early detection. That's why I'm recommending a larger budget for the Forest Service for back country patrols.

Austin observed, "I know I rarely get into the forest with all the paperwork. Seems I spend most of my time in the office or handling business with people."

Sam continued, "And as for fire, scientific studies point out that logged and roaded areas have much higher percentages of forest fires than undisturbed forests. Also, it won't hurt to let some forest fires alone to burn themselves out. After all, they are a part of the natural process and open up places in the forest. In fact, I'll bet this meadow right here was the scene of a small lightning fire a long time ago."

Spruce reflected on Austin's comments on the beetles. Over the years on several occasions, there had been attacks by small numbers of Engelmann spruce beetles on his bark. But, as a healthy and vigorous tree, Spruce had been able to resist them by letting sap flow out through the holes that they bored or by pitching them out. As a result, the beetles were caught in the sap or discouraged in their invasion. If a few did survive in his cambium layer, they could do little harm. And then the woodpeckers would usually peck those beetles and their larva out.

When it came to fires, Spruce remembered seeing more that a dozen small lightning fires from his overlook. They had usually burned out with pleasant, open spaces appearing here and there in the forest where they had been. These openings had later provided browse and cover for wildlife and were filled with wild flowers and new tree growth.

Spruce continued to listen to the controversial discussion of the party as they sat and talked around the campfire far into the night. On several occasions, Sam and Wagner had raised their voices to make a point in their arguments. Spruce observed that Congressman Vince Middleberry had said very little beyond questions to get more information, but that he was taking everything in.

At one point, Spruce was delighted to hear Heather say, "Sure, there are all kinds and forms of pressures for development of wilderness. And they all emphasize the dollars resulting and some local people benefitting from logging, mining and roads. But my Spruce over there has a right to live just like we all do. Pressures like this will always be here and they can go to plenty of other places. But not my Spruce. It can't!"

In the morning after a hearty breakfast of pancakes, sausage patties, and hot coffee, the congressional party began to break camp. Austin's plans for the field trip included four overnight camp outs so that they could get an overview of the entire area. Today, they would head up to a campsite on the tundra. Before leaving the meadow, Heather bid a warm farewell to Spruce and repeated her promise.

On slower horses traveling at the same pace, Vince and Heather turned out to be traveling companions between the rest of the party and the pack horse. To break the ice, Heather remarked, "You know, Vince, you certainly look a lot more relaxed now. I thought that you looked somewhat tense and tired when I first met you."

Smiling broadly, Vince shifted back and forth in his saddle and said, "Beyond some saddle soreness–haven't been on a horse in years–I feel great. All the cares and worries of Congress just seem to drop away out here. Hard to describe, but I do feel a lot better."

Heather returned the smile and asked, "Well, you certainly do look better, too. By the way, Vince, do you think there are any particular things that you would like to do in the wilderness?"

Vince replied, "Well, my wife and I do some bird watching around Washington, and I've been trying to do some out here. But, being out in this country for the first time, I've never seen most of the birds before."

Heather said, "I'm sort of an amateur birder. Maybe I can be of some help. In this mountain forest, we will be going through different ecological zones on our trip. With habitat requirements and ranges varying for different birds, we'll see some birds here in this spruce–fir or Taiga zone that we generally will not see when we get up in the tundra. And still others in areas below here in the montane zone with its lodgepole pine, quaking aspen, and ponderosa pine. In this spruce–fir area, I'm sure we'll see plenty of gray jays or camp robbers and Clark's nutcrackers–like the ones that were hanging around our camp yesterday–and lots of other kinds like Stellar's jay, red-breasted nuthatch, mountain chickadee, and.."

Vince shouted, "Look Heather! Look at that brightly colored bird that just landed in the tree on our right. Why it's absolutely gorgeous." Heather and Vince stopped their horses as they were captivated by the breathtaking beauty of the western tanager. The brilliant male was a lemon-yellow color with a red head and with black wings and tail. From its perch on a bough of subalpine fir, the striking bird sang a deliberate, robin-like song. Soon it flew off in its constant search for insects. Vince remarked, "I'll never forget the breathtaking beauty of that bird."

Heather identified the western tanager along with several other bird species as they continued along their way. Austin led the party along a well used game trail where few people had traveled. The trail was interwoven through the primeval forest of huge spruce and fir trees, which kept out much of the daylight. The enchanting atmosphere of the forest wonderland and its life seemed to cast a spell of natural fascination and mystery over the party. They all fell silent as if in deep thought and meditation about life itself.

Gradually, the trail started its swing upward toward the tundra as the horses began to climb slowly through a series of switchbacks. Contrasted to the large trees of the deep forest, the mountain slope trees followed a general pattern of gradually reduced size. More and more open places occurred along the trail as the party started to approach timberline.

Spellbound, the party stopped and scanned the rolling, large green meadows of tundra that lay before the rocks and snow of the mountaintops. In the distance, they could make out Gem Lake, a small, bright blue body of water that nestled in the alpine meadows like an odd-shaped sapphire set in the green velvet of a jewelry box. Although late in the season, many tundra flowers were still in bloom and gave a multi-colored effect to the expansive, charming meadowlands. The impact of the unique scene left the party silent and enthralled.

Sam broke the quiet and said, "How do you put something like this into a government report or congressional testimony–or into anything for that matter? I guess words are pretty ineffective for communicating some of the things on this trip."

Wagner started to reply, but then checked himself. Finally, Austin pointed toward the far end of the lake where they would camp for the night as the horses moved forward. Along the way, Heather identified a black rosy finch and white crowned sparrow for Vince. When they reached the lake, a large golden eagle suddenly appeared overhead as it soared away from them into the approaching sunset.

With the campsite set up, Heather suggested, "Vince, how about some fishing? There's still time to do some fly fishing before dark."

Vince laughed and replied, "Why, I've never been fly fishing in my life. Besides, I've never been very good at fishing even with worms and all sorts of lures."

Austin urged, "Go ahead and give it a try. There's some nice cutthroat trout in Gem Lake with little fishing pressure in a spot like this. I'll bet you do pretty good."

Reluctantly, Vince joined Heather as she rigged up fly fishing outfits for their outing. At the shore of the lake, Vince proceeded to entangle himself in fly line in two unsuccessful casts. Getting untangled with Heather's assistance, he managed to get his fly out about a dozen feet from the shoreline. Without warning, a large cutthroat grabbed the fly as it leaped high into the air. Thrilled and delighted, Vince frantically held onto the fly rod as the fish played and dashed here and there as line stripped from the reel. With excited coaching from the rest of the party, he played the trout until it settled down to running small circles in front of him. As it gradually tired, Heather slid her fingers under its gills and hoisted it onto the bank. Vince felt very proud as he carefully examined the two-pound trout with a bright red patch on its throat.

He remarked, "So that's how they get the name cutthroat trout–looks like his throat was bleeding."

Heather said, "We also call them natives. They are usually found in wild country like this, unlike stocked fish. C'mon, let's get some more." In a short time, the two anglers had a nice mess of trout for dinner.

After a delicious meal of fried trout, potatoes, and onions, the party settled around the campfire and continued their discussion about wilderness pros and cons. Sam indicated that his impressions of the area were that it was of high and unique wilderness character and that it should be classified as such. Wagner continued to voice his opinion that the area should be logged and developed. Vince remained generally quiet and noncommittal, but everyone could sense that he was deeply moved.

The party remained one more night at the campsite with side trips throughout the tundra. They then dropped down to lower elevations for four days and set up campsites at other locations, including the montane zone with its ponderosa pine and Lodgepole pine forests. There field trip had taken them throughout the entire ranges of the mountain forest of Grandview. They had been exposed to its unique features, natural beauty, and wild character from the streams and meadows of its lower portions to the highest point of its tundra and mountain lakes. In anticipation, the party now was ready for the public hearing at Big Log to find out that the public thought about the area and wilderness planning for it.

(9) THE PUBLIC HEARING

With his seniority on the Public Lands Committee, Congressman Vince Middleberry automatically became the chairman for conducting the public hearing at Big Log. Congressmen Sam Nelson and Wagner McPloiter were to assist him as members of the subcommittee on the Grandview field assignment. All three were seated behind a long table at the front of the high school auditorium at 8:30 in the morning as the people began to come in.

At first they were a little surprised to see such a nice and early turnout for a public hearing in a small town. But then they became astounded as the crowd continued to pour in and pack the entire auditorium. Congressman Middleberry estimated that there were more than 500 people in attendance with standing room only. He and the others quickly noticed that the majority had green tags with large "W"s attached to clothing.

At the entrance to the auditorium, Paul Spur and his father had set up a citizen action table. They had been very busy handing out the green tags and action summary sheets to wilderness supporters as they were about to enter the auditorium. Some of Paul's and Heather's high school friends, along with several of Professor Spur's students and faculty colleagues, were assisting at the action table. They had all driven down to Big Log from University City for the public hearing. When the hearing was about to begin, everyone went inside as Congressman Middleberry rose to address the excited audience.

Pounding his gavel several times, Congressman Middleberry started his introduction remarks as quiet and order gradually descended upon the people. After introductions, he said, "Well, folks, its very good to see such a large and unexpected turnout for this public hearing on whether or not the Grandview area of the Two Moon National Forest qualifies for wilderness study. As I am sure you know, a moratorium has been declared on the building of logging roads and logging operations in the area until this question has been decided. My Congressional colleagues and I have recently completed a week-long field trip in the area to gain on-the-spot information and impressions. And now we would like to hear your opinions on the matter. With this and future information from the Forest Service, we will then make our recommendations to the Public Lands Committee of Congress. So let us begin."

Looking at the long list of people who had signed up to testify, the Congressmen realized that they would be lucky to complete the public hearing by nightfall. Restricting the testimony time to five minutes with written statements to be submitted for elaboration, Congressman Middleberry called the first witness who was the Governor of the state.

Governor Ted Smith, a politician who had a lot of connections with industry, told the gathering that he had received a great deal of communication on the issue from the national and state public with most of it urging the wilderness position. At the same time, he also said that he had responsibilities to the state's economy and to motorized recreation for the area. As a result, he felt that he could not endorse wilderness that would lock up the area from development and motorized recreation but he could recommended a compromise.

In describing the compromise, Governor Smith said, "Why not keep parts of it wild and roadless while developing those parts that have economic and motorized recreational potential by having the Forest Service Zone them. We do not need an unnecessary wilderness designation to do this." He went on to mention several parts for development that would include more than two-thirds of the Grandview–one of which contained Spruce's location.

Congressman Nelson asked, "But Governor Smith, every bit of the Grandview area may have potential with enough economic and motorized recreation pressures. What guarantees would there be that even your small wild parts would not eventually be developed?"

Governor Smith replied, "If future decisions on those parts had to be made, I am sure that we could rely on the Forest Service, with the help of state and local officials as well as the business community, to decide what was in the public interest for their development or preservation."

Congressman Nelson cynically remarked, "I'm sure they would! I have no further questions on your noble compromise, Governor."

The next witness called was the Mayor of Big Log, Conrad Burnaby, who noted his strong opposition to any form of wilderness for the Grandview area. As the owner of a local bar and service station, he protested that the whole economy and welfare of Big Log depended on having the area opened up for logging and roading. "We are for progress and for the future in this town–not for stagnation through tying up our rich timber resources for some nature lovers to hike in," Burnaby said. "And the logging roads can be improved and used by plenty of people with ATVs and snowmobiles. Our town would greatly benefit from a flourishing business like this. After all, National Forest should serve the interests of the local communities and not be locked up."

The mayor was followed by the regional representative of the Sierra Club, Dr. Beal Mossman, who said, "Public lands, like this national forest, belong to all the people of the United States. A citizen from Cleveland, Ohio, has just as much claim on this area as a citizen of Big Log. Decisions on how to use a given national forest must be based on the national public interest. In this case, the highest and wisest use of the area would be wilderness. Congressmen, I call your attention to the tremendous amount of public response for wilderness designation of this area. And this response has come from all over the nation, as well as from the people of this state. In joining with the Wilderness Society, Alliance for the Wild Rockies, and many other environmental organizations, we of the Sierra Club submit that this unique and scenic area highly qualifies for wilderness and that it should be designated as such."

Congressman Middleberry called as next witness, Ruford Plank, the President of the Happy Motor Recreation Club which, was part of the "Multiple Use" coalition financed by American and Japanese motorized corporations. President Plank testified, "I am representing over 300 people in this state who use and enjoy the great outdoors and this national forest through motorcycles, ATVs, four wheel drives, and snowmobiles. We oppose any wilderness designation for this area because we are prohibited from using our motorized vehicles in wilderness areas. By the way, can I ask one of you congressmen why we are prohibited in wilderness?

Congressman Nelson volunteered, "The Wilderness Act of 1964 clearly states that motorized equipment of any type is not permitted in designated wilderness areas. Vehicles like motorcycles, ATVs, and four wheel drives and snowmobiles are simply incompatible with the purposes of the Act, which is keep the wilderness areas under their primeval character and natural conditions and to avoid any signs and indications of civilization such as the presence, noise, and disturbance of motorized vehicles.

The club President angrily retorted, "But what harm do we do? We have just as much right as any hiker to be up there!"

Congressman Nelson calmly replied, "Not according to my observations. For example, your motorized vehicles leave large ruts in fragile areas which destroy natural vegetation and cause erosion. Snowmobiles, for example, pack down the insulating snow and

kill the unprotected plant life underneath. They also disturb wildlife when they are in a weakened winter condition. I can show you
many reports of wildlife deaths resulting from harassment by
snowmobilers. And then there is the air and water pollution, not
to mention the noise pollution of the vehicles that simply ruins
the wilderness experience for others. I believe the prohibiting of
motorized vehicles and equipment is well founded for wilderness
considerations. After all, you and other motorized people already
have the far greater portions of national forests open for your type
of recreation. Why not let a small portion of wilderness remain
undisturbed?"

Enraged, the club President Plank shouted, "This is a democ-
racy, Mr. Politician, and we should be allowed to run our vehicles
where we want to and when we want to!"

Over two dozen other motor club members in the audience
also started shouting in unison as Congressman Middleberry
brought the gavel down hard several times. In a loud and firm
voice, he said, "Anymore outbursts like this, and I will terminate
this hearing. You are dismissed as a witness, sir."

As the club President stomped back to his seat, Congressman
Nelson reflected on him. He wondered if the man had ever experi-
enced the solitude and quiet of a wilderness experience without
his mechanical toys. He speculated that the man might just be
afraid of wilderness, yet was obsessed with the need to conquer it
through noise and technology. He started to realize more and more
that the club president and people like him could simply not stand
to let any area alone in its free and wild state. If anything, it appeared that these wild areas held a special fascination to be conquered with their machines.

All three Congressman were very aware of something unusual
at this hearing as compared to other public hearings in the field.
There was an unusual proportion of young people present, and
they were testifying as individuals or as representatives of organizations that contained young people. Outing clubs, 4-H clubs,
photography clubs, and other groups from high schools in Univer-

sity City and nearby towns were heavily represented at the meeting as being in favor of wilderness for the area. The young people
brought a unique idealism, freshness, and sincerity to the hearing.
Many of them had been reached through Heather and Paul in
their talks, email, and telephone calls.

When Congressman McPloiter asked one of the young people
why he was testifying, the Vice President of an outing club, Jay
Kirkpatrick, replied, "Sir, after many of you older people are gone,
we, of my generation, will have to live with what you have decided
to do or not to do in this area. And we want to do everything we
can to insure that it is not irreversibly developed, but kept forever
wild for future generations to enjoy. The more that your generation decides to develop, the less that there will for our generation
as well as future generations to decide and enjoy. So I decided to
get involved. Congressman, this is the first time that I really feel
like an American citizen. It's not a matter of how old we are, but
how we are affected and involved."

When Heather and Paul testified, they brought in the wilderness values that were hammered out over the campfire with their
father. They pointed out that the area provided the opportunity
for youth to gain solid values through exposure to wild country.
Heather devoted a part of her testimony to telling about Spruce.
She simply talked about the beautiful tree and its natural setting
of the meadow and mountain forest and what it meant to her. The
Congressmen leaned forward in rapt attention as the audience silently listened in awe. Heather conveyed her love for Spruce and
the area to the group and brought out some of the deep values and
intangibles of the entire issue. There was a long pause after she
concluded her testimony with many people moved by her words.

After a short lunch break, the public meeting continued until
early evening. Many witnesses, representing themselves or their
organizations, had testified for or against wilderness for the area.
They had ranged from Mr. Quincy Sawyer, the owner of a local
sawmill to the executive director of the Wilderness Society. High
school and college students, outfitters, mining engineers, house-

wives, doctors, company foresters, professional environmentalists, construction executives, teachers, and a host of other people made up the wide variety of witnesses on either side. Besides testifying themselves, the Spur family had been very active in getting people and organizations to testify or to send in a written statement of support. Many environmental organizations had quickly alerted their members to the cause.

As a result, all three congressmen were impressed with the support for wilderness from the great majority of people at the meeting as well as the numbers that many of them represented. The minority against wilderness had tried desperately but could not muster the numbers or strength to offset that support as much as they tried.

Congressman Middleberry finally concluded the meeting after hearing the last witness. it was obvious to almost everyone present that the meeting had overwhelmingly been in favor of wilderness. But Congressman McPloiter quickly remarked to his colleagues, "This is a bunch of baloney with too many irrational and emotional people here. And most of them are not from this local community. I've never believed in this public participation junk anyway. And I'm sure that Congress will handle it much more rationally by taking care of the real interests and the local economy involved here."

As soon as the opportunity presented itself, the Spurs met with Congressman Nelson. Professor Spur asked, "What now, Sam?"

He replied, "Well, Frank, I think that we have some strong points and support now. We can go three ways. One, we now have plenty of ammunition, particularly public support, to pressure the chief of the Forest Service to order a wilderness study. Two, I could try to introduce legislation through the Public Lands Committee of Congress to legally order the Forest Service to do the wilderness study. Three, I could introduce legislation through the same committee to get the area declared instant wilderness through a Congressional bill. But a lot depends on how the Public Lands Committee reacts to our report when we get back."

Professor Spur commented, "That last alternative of instant wilderness really appeals to me. If the Forest Service is pressured or legislated into a wilderness study, I do get the impression that there would be a lot of static and resistance from them. Besides, they have a tendency to cut or discourage a lot of legitimate wilderness out of any area to accommodate every conceivable use under the sun, particularly with a lot of local pressure from logging and motorized recreation. What do you think we should do?"

Sam replied, "At this point, I would suggest pressuring the Forest Service. The national attention that you people started rolling over a month ago still has the Forest Service nervous. But real effective pressure could come through the Public Lands Committee. And Congressman Middleberry could be a key factor in all this. Most of the committee really listens to him. By the way, he and Heather got on very well on the trip. They were just like old wilderness buddies."

Heather smiled and said, "I really liked him once I got to know him better. I just know that he loves that area and would like to see it stay the way it is. I somehow feel that he picked up a real understanding, feeling, and love for wilderness on the trip."

Sam said, "I sure hope so, Heather, but it is certainly hard to get any commitment from him on it. With his power on the committee, we'd even have a good chance to get through instant wilderness legislation if he were to sponsor it. But. . . ."

Paul interrupted, "Say, how about if Heather asked him to write and introduce a bill like that? Maybe he would listen to her."

Sam turned to Heather and asked, "How about it, Heather? Do you want to try?"

"O.K." Heather replied.

As Congressman Middleberry was making some notes alone on the public hearing, Heather asked to see him for a moment. Smiling, he beckoned her to a chair and said, "Hi, Heather. By the way, that was a great testimony that you presented."

"Thank you very much. Vince, how does it look?"

Well, I'm in the process of writing up my report on the field trip and public hearing and will still have to confer with my colleagues and the Forest Service. But there seems to be a pretty strong case made for wilderness consideration of the area, including the interest shown by young people like yourself. But I've been in Congress too long to predict how things will finally turn out."

Heather then asked, "But, Vince, how do you feel about it? I just know that trip meant so much to you!"

He hesitated several moments while he tried to sort out his thoughts for her soul searching question. Finally he gave up and blurted out, "Heather, that trip did mean more to me than anything I've done for some time. I never felt so alive in all my life. I just could not believe that such magnificent country still existed. I want to go back there again and take my family with me. I love that wild, wonderful place. Why I . . ."

The Congressman stopped himself. He had an embarrassed– but relieved–expression on his face as if he had said something that he wanted to say for some time.

Heather and Vince continued to look at each other until she remarked, "Vince, Sam thinks there is a good chance for making the area an instant wilderness if you would introduce a bill like this in your committee. Could you do this?"

Startled, Vince fell into silence. As the astute, but compromising politician that he was, Vince hesitated to make any form of commitment. Finally, he said, "Heather, you are really putting me on the spot today. To be perfectly honest, I've never thought of this possibility. I know that my colleagues in Congress would never expect something like an instant wilderness bill from myself. I just don't know what to say at this point. Give me a chance to think it over."

(10) CONGRESSIONAL HEARINGS

After the Congressmen arrived back in Washington, D.C., they were scheduled to make their report to the Public Lands Committee in five days. When they met informally over lunch to go over the report, Vince boldly announced, "I have decided to introduce a bill that would make the Grandview Area an instant wilderness." Sam beamed with a broad smile while Wagner grimaced as he let a glass fall out of his hand.

Wagner exclaimed, "You can't do this! Besides being an action which is wrong, we were sent out there by the Public Lands Committee to come back with a report. We were not sent out there to come up with a Congressional bill. Why, Vince, I'm very shocked and disappointed in you."

With a calm and determined expression on his face, Vince said, "Well, look at the Constitutional Convention in Philadelphia over two centuries ago. They were supposed to come up with a report and recommendations for Congress and they came up with a whole new Constitution. I don't see why . . ."

Wagner interrupted, "This is no joking matter. If you try this,

I'll see the bill killed before it gets anywhere. And you know that I can bring plenty of pressure from Congress and our lumber and mining industries, not to mention those motorized "multiple use" groups, to shoot this ridiculous legislation down. Vince, what's wrong with you?"

Vince replied, "Nothing. I'm just doing what the public interest and my conscience dictates for me to do on the matter."

Throwing down his napkin, Wagner stomped out of the room as he angrily said, "We'll see about that!"

Sam said, "Vince, good show! But, I'll bet Wagner will see to it that every lumber and mining lobbyist knows about this right away. And those motorized recreation people are getting more and more powerful and financed. Do you think we can really swing it with both the House and Senate besides the committee? As we both know, instant wilderness legislation like this is going to need tremendous support."

Vince replied, "Well, I'm betting on it. I slept on it for a couple of nights and made up my mind to go ahead. You know, Sam, I really believe in this–I discovered–thanks to Heather. By the way, I've already done some groundwork on this."

Sam studied Vince. He had never seen the man so fired up about legislation before. He knew that Vince had introduced few bills during his years in Congress, and plenty of Congressmen owed him support for backing their legislation. Sam listened carefully as Vince continued, "I've talked Senator Jack McMaster into introducing a companion bill into his Natural Resources Committee. His bill will be identical to the one I'll be introducing into the Public Lands Committee in the House. As chairman of the committee, Jack should be able to get it through with little difficulty. If both committees approve the identical bills, it will really speed up the process of getting everything done on the floor of the House and Senate–provided we get the support we need."

Sam commented, "Sounds great, Vince. I know we'll get plenty of opposition from Wagner in the Committee and on the house flour. We sure will need all the support we can get from our colleagues and the public. I'll get on the telephone and tell the Spurs your good news and call for their action. And then start alerting all the environmental organizations nationwide for support. And then . . ."

Vince interrupted, "I've already called Heather. She promised that they would get right on it. If the environmental organizations and those young people can bring some of that national public opinion to bear on Congress, we should really be in the ball game."

Sam said, "If it's going to work, they'll have to get an avalanche of letters, emails, telegrams, and telephone calls of support to Congress right away. Otherwise, those logging and mining and motorized lobbyists will get to lambast it first with little opposition. I sure hope the public comes through on this."

At University City, the Spurs were busily engaged in reaching every individual and organization they could think of. They wrote or called potentially interested parties around the city, state, and nation and asked them, to get in touch with their Congressmen on the instant wilderness legislation.

While doing this, Paul remembered an exchange student, William Switzer, from Switzerland, who had joined the Spur family on one of their hiking trips to the Grandview area. The young Swiss had fallen in love with the back country there and vowed that he would return someday. Paul and William had corresponded off and on since his return to high school in Switzerland. Suddenly an idea hit Paul and he said, "Say, Dad, how about getting some international support on this–like William Switzer?"

Professor Spur responded, "That might not hurt at all. It would certainly be a bit unusual, but worth trying. What do you think, Heather?"

Stopping her emailing of a letter to the National Girl Scout headquarters for a moment, Heather replied, "I know William will come through. Maybe Paul could ask him to contact some conservation organizations in Europe to write, too."

Paul said, "Why not! Congress is usually pretty sensitive to public opinion from other countries. I'll get a email letter off to

William right away. Been meaning to write him anyway. Hey, there goes the telephone again. I'll get it."

Since the launching of their wilderness campaign for the Grandview, many environmental organizations had maintained close communications with them by telephone, email, and correspondence. This call from, Marilyn Beech, a staff officer of the Wilderness Society in Washington, D.C., informed Paul and the others that the lumber industries and Congressman Wagner McPloiter were pressing Congress and the Forest Service to drop the moratorium on logging at the Grandview area as soon as possible.

Marilyn said, "We are really worried about this. It could mean immediate construction of the logging roads with logging operations starting right away. Congressman McPloiter is getting support from congressmen who have political commitments or sympathy with lumber and mining industries. This could sabotage the efforts for the wilderness legislation. Can you people do anything to help on this?"

Paul replied, "Gosh, we are already working very hard to contact every group and individual that we know or can think of–everywhere–even in Switzerland. We don't see how we can do much more."

Then Marilyn said, "I'm sure you people are doing everything possible as we are. Right now, we are sending out instant alerts on this to our entire membership. But, somehow, we have to reach as much as possible of the American public right away. Your family really got this whole thing started and called a lot of public attention to it.'

Pausing, Marilyn asked, "How about appearing on national TV to call it to the public's attention again? One of our members is the vice president of a major national TV network with coast-to-coast coverage. He could have a TV team sent to your home for an interview right away. What do you say?"

After an immediate family conference, Paul answered, "Sure, we'll be glad to do it. But I do think that we should make a special appeal to young people to write to their congressman on it."

Marilyn responded, "That's fine with me. O.K., I'll get right on it."

The next day a TV crew arrived at the Spur household. Some of the photographs of the Grandview area, including one of Spruce, were captured on TV. The Spur family made comments on the wilderness heritage and values of the area as well as the need to protect it through legislation. They discussed the threat of logging, roads, and other developments and urged everyone to write their Congressman to support the instant wilderness legislation. Professor Spur suggested that some could start petitions and get plenty of signatures on them for sending to Congress besides the email, letters, and telegrams.

During the TV interview, Paul said, "It's about time for young people like you and me to get involved in something like this. Otherwise, we will not have a voice in determining what kind of a world we will be living in—now or in the future. The decisions will be made by some people and politicians who put dollars and power first and who could care less about our wilderness and environmental quality. And we have a right to determine our own future as citizens, regardless of our age."

Heather Said, "That's right It's up to you. The fate of this beautiful wilderness area really is in your hands. Do you want to see it protected or ruined? You will have to live with the results of what Congress decides on the Grandview. So please get busy and write to your Congressman today." Shortly afterwards, their taped TV interview appeared nationwide during news reports.

Back in Washington, D.C., Congressman Vince Middleberry and Senator Jack McMaster were introducing their identical instant wilderness legislation to their respective committees. As soon as Congressman Middleberry had introduced the bill, Congressman McPloiter voiced a strong objection and said, "On behalf of many of my congressional colleagues and constituents, I wish to indicate my total opposition to this unreasonable and unnecessary legislation. As the committee members will recall, Congressman Nelson, Congressman Middleberry, the author of this absurd legislation, and I were dispatched by this committee to make a report on the area through a field trip and public hearing. Certainly not to come up with new legislation like this. I consider Congressman Middleberry's action to be premature and unfounded and request that the Committee immediately disregard it."

The Chairman of the committee, Congressman Robert Jonas, studied his committee for several moments before replying. He tried to fit this into his general position of being a compromiser with an economic development bent. He knew that Congressman McPloiter had supporters in and outside the committee in Congress; they had backed him on his efforts in trying to terminate the moratorium on logging.

But, email, telephone calls, letters and telegrams were pouring into Congress like an avalanche with the request that Grandview be declared a wilderness. Congressman Jonas tried to avoid controversies that would cause problems on the committee. yet he knew he was really getting into one now, particularly after watching the TV news last night and the Spur family. And the strong involvement of young people made him feel uncomfortable about their power and influence. Many Congressmen had already approached him and reported the massive communications that they were already getting about this issue from their constituents. He felt that he would to play this one very carefully.

Finally, Chairman Jonas said, "Congressman McPloiter, I believe we all know that Congressman Middleberry is within his rights in introducing this legislation to this committee–which will give its full consideration and study to it. I also believe that Congressmen Middleberry and Nelson and yourself will be able to present the field and public hearing report, including differing opinions, along with the proposed legislation. Now, gentlemen, we have a number of items to cover on our agenda so I suggest that we move right along to other business. The legislation for instant wilderness designation of the Grandview area and discussion on the termination of the logging moratorium for it will be postponed to a future meeting."

As Congressmen Middleberry and Nelson left the committee meeting three hours later, Sam remarked, "That sly, old fox, Jonas. I'll just bet he keeps stalling around and postponing your legislation for the rest of the session until the public clamor dies down. Those committee chairmen can do what they want, regardless of what the public wants."

Vince agreed, "I'm sure that he'll try. He's got a hot one on his hands, but he knows that public attention on any issue does not last long and people do forget quickly. That's why it took 10 years to get the Wilderness Act of 1964 through Congress after it was introduced in 1954, despite strong public opinion. Say, let's go over to the Senate and see how Senator Jack McMaster is coming along with his Grandview bill."

With a confident smile, Senator McMaster welcomed them into his office, and said, "I think we're in good shape on my committee, particularly with all this nationwide publicity coming in on it. Some committee members immediately objected, but I expected this since those particular people get a lot of their campaign funds from lumber and mining industries. But every senator that I know has received plenty of response from his constituents urging him to support the legislation. And that TV coverage of the Spur family should bring a lot more. Even my Senate colleagues from Eastern and Southern states are getting plenty of mail on this. And the interesting thing is that much of this is coming from young people. The letters that I have received from them are filled with a very personal and sincere concern for the wilderness protection of Grandview. They really grab me. With this kind of support, I don't see too many problems in getting it through my committee and the Senate."

As the two Congressmen were walking back to the House office buildings Sam said, 'Vince, according to Jack, the Senate side looks pretty good. But our Public Lands Committee, through Jonas and Wagner, could delay it until almost everybody forgets about it. And have you seen all the anti-wilderness advertisements by the lumber and mining and the motorized recreation industries that are suddenly appearing in the newspapers and on TV? With our slow-acting committee that stuff could kill the public support. We need to get the bill through now."

Vince responded, "I don't believe the American public is going to be fooled by phony advertisements of corporations, not the way they believe in wilderness. Also, we now have growing public response to support moving the bill up as a priority item in committee. And I'm sure we will have a lot more when the committee meets on Monday."

Meanwhile, back at University City, Paul received an email from Switzerland. William Switzer wrote, "I am very glad that you called my attention to the plight of our favorite hiking place which I remember so well. I feel that places like this are a natural heritage of all citizens of our planet earth—not just to the country where they happen to be located. Ecologically and spiritually, wilderness is our heritage, regardless of where it is and what country we are from. We all have a responsibility to protect such unique and beautiful places wherever they are. Members of my outing club and I have written letters on saving Grandview as wilderness to your leaders in Congress. And we have contacted the World Conservation Union in Gland, Switzerland, and they are cooperating with us in calling this matter to the attention of environmental organizations all over the world. You should soon have a lot of support from many nations to your Congress. Hope this will be of definite help."

When Congressman Jonas had dismissed the last Committee meeting, he was confident that the Grandview Instant Wilderness Bill could be postponed indefinitely until it finally died in committee after the public uproar diminished. Two of his campaign contributors from the lumber industry, along with some Congressmen, had even congratulated him on his strategy.

But now he was not so sure as he started to open the Monday meeting with the bill not even on the agenda. Too many Congressmen had contacted him about the increased volume of correspondence and communications that they were getting on the bill with the larger percentage coming from young people. He also felt increasingly uncomfortable with numerous, foreign environmental organizations from joining in support. Even the State Department was involved through environmental contacts to their embassies.

He had also received a tremendous amount of communications directed at himself. The teenage son of a Director of National Parks from a developing nation wrote, "You, in the United States, expect us to set aside wilderness areas to save endangered wildlife and tropical forests. And we are trying to do this, despite a large population and poor economy. But, with a rich and large nation like yours, certainly you can afford to protect and preserve a few wilderness areas like the Grandview."

This young man had embarrassed him, but the telephone call from a top aide in the White House had really worried him. The aide had said, "The President has had a great deal of communications on this matter. As you know, he is very concerned about his image with the public–both national and international–not to mention the young people involved. Consequently, he strongly urges you to move ahead on the legislation."

When Congressman Jonas mentioned that the Forest Service had indicated its opposition to the bill, the aide said, "I am sure that you are aware that the man in the office next to mine also runs the Forest Service. You can count on the support of the Administration for this legislation."

As Congressman Jonas nervously called the meeting to order, he could easily see that the entire membership had been under a great deal of pressure from the public, their constituents and their colleagues. He knew that sticking to the agenda would be futile and damaging at this point. Finally, he said, "Gentlemen, in view of the high amount of interest shown in the Grandview Instant Wilderness Legislation, I propose that we consider it as a priority item and move it to the top of our agenda for preliminary discussion. Are there any objections?"

Congressman McPloiter wanted to object, but remained silent. Even his supporters on the committee had warned him that something had to be done.

With this, the committee process on the controversial legislation had begun. To start the ball rolling, the Chairman asked Congressmen Middleberry, McPlointer, and Nelson to make a report on their field trip and public hearing as it related to the legislation. He was careful to limit the time on this matter and then switched back to the regular agenda. But being very aware of the tense situation, he set up a series of committee hearings on the bill that would permit representatives from industrial and environmental sides to testify. Realizing that he had no alternative, he had at least "saved face" to a degree under the circumstances. Chairman Jonas breathed a sigh of relief as they continued through other items on the agenda.

At the Senate Committee on Natural Resources, Senator McMaster steered his almost identical bill gracefully through the committee hearing process as a priority item. Given large financial backing, lobbyists for the lumber and mining and motorized recreation industries were only able to hold a minority of the committee as a virtual landslide of public support for the bill flooded the members. One month after its introduction, the Senate committee, with a strong majority vote, sent it to the Senate floor with a recommendation for "Do Pass." With Senator McMaster and the majority leader championing its cause, the Senate passed the bill with a vote of 86 for and 12 against. with two abstentions.

Public opnion then centered on Congressman Jonas' Committee as the House Bill continued through committee hearings. At the same time, lumber industries ran full page ads that said the Grandview wilderness legislation was a test case that could ruin the industry by locking up America. Congressman McPloiter, realizing that he could not stop the legislation, introduced a series of crippling amendments that would greatly reduce the wilderness area. When this failed, he proposed another amendment that would provide for a corridor with a highway through the middle of it. If implemented, the highway would have demolished Spruce and his meadow.

But the environmental organizations, along with the Spur family, had caused a virtual tidal wave of public opinion to descend on the committee and Congress. Even Congressman McPloiter's strongest supporters in Congress told him that they could not back his amendments with this type of public support.

After four months of hearings–public, Congressional, and Presidential–pressure continued to bear strongly on the committee to get the bill to the House floor. The Speaker of the House warned Congressman Jonas that delaying it any further would only cause very serious problems. The Speaker asked, "Does your committee think you can take on the American public–and now the international public?"

Congressman Jonas knew that he would lose some of his campaign contributions from lumber and mining industries by taking positive action. But he also realized that he would really hurt his political and public standing by continuing on this delaying path. Finally, he told the Speaker, "O.K., I'll do something about it."

At the next committee meeting, the chairman brought the bill up for a vote. With the exception of congressman McPloiter and two others, everyone on the committee voted for its passage. Then, with a great deal of help from their colleagues, Congressmen Middleberry and Nelson carried on a vigorous campaign for the bill on the House floor.

When the vote was taken, the Grandview Wilderness Act passed the House with 399 for and 30 against with 6 abstentions. It was the first time since anyone could remember that every member of the House of Representatives had shown up to vote all at once. Both the Senate and House bills were so similar that little had to be done in a conference committee. The President anxiously signed the Bill and then gave a short TV speech on the power and dedication of young people and international interest in wilderness.

Shortly afterwards, Congressman Middleberry called Heather and said, "We did it, Heather! A lot of hard work on all of our parts, but the Grandview Wilderness Area, including your beloved Wilderness Spruce, will be there in perpetuity for present and future generations to enjoy. This will make Grandview a permanent part of our National Wilderness System. Congratulations!'

It was in early summer that Spruce happily witnessed the Spur family making their way toward the meadow with Tommi Wing, the new Grandview district ranger. Austin Miller had been promoted to Deputy Forest Supervisor in another national forest. This time, Gloria Spur, the teenagers' mother, had joined them.

When they reached the meadow, Heather ran to Spruce and exclaimed, "Spruce, I kept my promise! We all worked hard and now you are an official part of the Grandview Wilderness Area and you don't have to ever worry about getting logged. You can live out your life here in this protected area. Listen, my beautiful Wilderness Spruce, I'm going to read a passage of the Wilderness Act that now includes you and the Grandview area of 390,000 acres of mountain forest."

Heather read, "A wilderness, in contract with those areas where man and his works dominate the landscape, is hereby recognized as an area where the earth and its community of life are untrammeled by man, where man is himself a visitor who does not remain. An area of wilderness is further defined to mean in this Act as an area of undeveloped Federal land retaining its primeval character and influence, without permanent improvements or human habitation, which is protected and managed so as to preserve its natural conditions and which (1) generally appears to have been affected primarily by the forces of nature, with the imprint of man's work substantially unnoticeable; (2) has outstanding opportunities for solitude or a primitive and unconfined type of recreation; (3) has at least five thousand acres of land or is of sufficient as to make practicable its preservation and use in an unimpaired condition; and (4) may also contain ecological, geological, or other features of scientific, educational, scenic, or historical value."

A wild and free life would now be secure for Wilderness Spruce and his offspring in perpetuity.

(THE END)

ABOUT THE AUTHOR

Daniel H. Henning, Ph.D. is Professor Emeritus of Political Science and Environmental Affairs and Distinguished Scholar Professor, Montana State University, Billings and Visiting Professor, Flathead Lake Biological Research Station, University of Montana. A past Senior Fulbright Research Scholar for South East Asia (tropical forests), he has presented a number of environmental papers at international conferences and meetings in Asia and Europe and has written numerous books and articles in the environmental field, including MANAGING THE ENVIRONMENTAL CRISIS (Duke University Press, 1999), BUDDHISM AND DEEP ECOLOGY (2001) and TREE TALK AND TALES.

He is the recipient of numerous honors and travel awards from the Smithsonian Institution (India); National Science Foundation (Malaysia and India); National Academy of Science Inter-Academy Exchange For Visiting Scientist (Czechoslovakia); Albert Einstein World Science Award Interdisciplinary Committee; Resources For the Future Fellowship; Ernest Swift Memorial Fellowship, National Wildlife Federation; Norwegian Marshall Fund Fellowship; World Who's Who in the World Environment; Outstanding Educators of America; Vice Chancellor's Faculty Award, Chinese University of Hong Kong; etc.

He has served on the World Conservation Union (IUCN) Commission on Education and Training and on their International Council of Environmental Law. Dr. Henning has chaired environmental training sessions for the American Society for Public Administration and is a member of the International Society of Tropical Foresters, the International Society for Tropical Ecology (India), the Sierra Club, Audubon Society, Natural Resources Defense Council, Alliance for the Wild Rockies, Friends of the Wild Swan, Native Forest Network, Earth Island Institute, and Natural Resources Defense Council.

Professor Henning has served as a park ranger naturalist in Glacier, Yellowstone, and Rocky Mountain National Parks and as a wilderness ranger in western national forests. Over the past twelve years, he has worked as a protected area/biodiversity consultant and trainer for the United Nations in Asia, including Cambodia, Thailand, and Myanmar (Burma), and also Norwegian and Australian National Parks. This experience included studying and working with Buddhism, Deep Ecology, and tropical forests in Asia and often living in Buddhist Forest Monasteries, including his being an ordained Buddhist Monk in Myanmar (Burma). He has completed a UNEP study on the ecological, forest, and environmental teachings of Buddha and was invited by H.H. The Dalai Lama to participate in the Ecological Responsibility Conference in India.

In his travels, Dr. Henning has conducted numerous presentations and workshops about forests, biodiversity, Buddhism, Deep Ecology, and environmental affairs. They included the World Fellowship of Buddhism, the World Wilderness Congress, the University of Oslo, the University of Montana, the American Center of United States Embassy, Myanmar, the University of Forestry, Myanmar, etc. He is currently consulting, conducting workshops and seminars, and doing volunteer work to help bring Buddhism and Deep Ecology into tropical forest protection in Asia during the winters and to protect old growth temperate forests of Montana and the West during his summers in that part of the world, through his life dedication to trees and forests.

Printed in the United States
731400001B